WOMEN, LANGUAGE & POWER

Giving Voice to Our Ambition

Susannah Baldwin, Ph.D.

Roaring Fork Press
San Francisco, California
susannahbaldwin.com

Library of Congress Cataloging-in-Publication has been applied for:

ISBN 978-1-7378105-0-6

Book cover, illustrations, and design by Craig Frazier
Edited by Kelly Griego
Copy edited by Katy Lindenmuth

Names and identifying characteristics of clients throughout the book have been changed to preserve their anonymity.

For my daughters, Jess and Sofia

Contents

Foreword

It is only recently that society has begun to appreciate that women have a right to speak and be heard privately, but especially publicly. The increasing presence and prominence of women in positions of power—positions in which we must be listened to and our utterances acted upon—is evidence that the millennia-old taboo against women's speech is finally eroding. But now that we have demonstrated that we have voices and the right to use them, how can we use them most effectively and achieve communicative power?

Susannah Baldwin has been using her considerable skills as a leader, teacher, coach, and communicator for many years to explore and address these questions. *Women, Language, and Power* represents the distillation of her work to expand women's power through the strategic use of language. The book will help you learn why women tend to speak the way they do, when this style serves women, and when it's wise to reach for new language choices. Through the research and resources Susannah provides in *Women, Language, and Power*, you will learn the most important thing that an able and ambitious woman needs to know: how to get things done through words.

Robin Tolmach Lakoff, Ph.D.
Author and professor of linguistics at the University of California, Berkeley

Acknowledgments

There are a handful of people without whom this book would have remained only a good idea.

Thank you

Kelly Griego: For your commitment to and talent for helping me refine and articulate my ideas, making this book a rich and more powerful tool for women. For your beautiful writing, your clarity on foggy Saturday morning calls, and your temperament throughout. Thank you for taking this journey with me.

David Baldwin: For your unwavering faith that my *Women, Language, and Power* workshop could become a book of substance. For your help weaving together material from my workshop, research articles, and long conversations into a first draft. Thank you for your intellectual rigor, collaboration, and extensive editing.

Michael Baldwin: For your generous encouragement and support, mastery of visual communication, and the gift of a PowerPoint deck for my first *Women, Language, and Power* workshop. Thank you for bringing my ideas to life.

Craig Frazier: For how you listen and how you see. Your unique ability to balance design and detail without sacrificing beauty brought additional depth and meaning to this book. Thank you for the magnificent cover, illustrations, and typography design.

Paul Good: For your tireless and invaluable editing, cheerleading, and mentoring. I am so much more, and I have accomplished so much more, because of you. Thank you for telling me to ride my own wave but always remaining by my side in support.

Katy Lindenmuth: For bringing your exacting eye to these pages. I have that much more confidence knowing that not an Oxford comma was missed, a modifier was left to dangle, or an errant space went undetected. Thank you for your copy edits and thoughtful content improvements.

Kathy Reddick and Melissa Daimler: For being such generous champions of my work. You opened so many doors, and so wide, for me. Thank you for all the opportunities.

Jess and Sofia Good: For cheering me on and promoting the *Women, Language, and Power* workshop. Thank you for your love and encouragement.

Robin Lakoff: For paving the way. Thank you for inspiring so many of us.

All the incredible women with whom I have had the privilege to work—and those who found their way to this book: Thank you for giving my work meaning and purpose. This book is for you.

WOMEN, LANGUAGE, AND POWER

PART 1

Losing Our Language

Overcoming the Cultural Constraints
That Undermine Women's Career
Advancement

A Note on Part One

If you are a woman reading this book, I know you. We may have never met, but I promise I know the difficulties you experience as a woman trying to progress in today's professional world—a world that remains predominantly run by men, with biases toward male leadership and barriers to women's advancement. I know how hard you work and how much you have to tolerate to work within this environment.

I know this because I have worked with so many women like you, who are trying to make it into management and leadership roles and confronting barriers and frustrated ambitions along the way. As a clinical psychologist who works as a communications and leadership coach to individual clients and teaches workshops to large groups of women, I have listened to scores of women share their professional aspirations, fears, hard pursuit of advancement, and disappointment when it doesn't come for reasons they either don't agree with or don't understand.

The conversation about the forces that challenge women's ability to rise to leadership levels, earn salaries commensurate with those of their male counterparts, and break the glass ceiling tends to focus on institutional barriers. This conversation is critical, as the more light we can shine on the structural forces that unfairly hold women back, the closer we can come to eliminating them once and for all. However, my lens as a communication coach has allowed me to see another force hindering women's advancement—one that women have the capacity to influence and change today: how they use language.

Over the course of my career, I have observed women at all levels of management and leadership communicating in corporate environments. I have seen strong communication skills accelerate careers—and weak communication skills stall them. The ability to leverage communication to influence, inspire, and build alliances requires a high level of skill and confidence in the public arena. Women who have mastered these skills gain power and thus feel powerful. Women who have not yet mastered these skills are often missing the biggest piece of the puzzle.

Women have been conditioned to communicate in a style that can undermine their power and effectiveness at work, ultimately thwarting their advancement. Through no fault of their own, they have been socialized to speak and behave in ways that are antithetical to what is necessary to advance in most corporations. Women develop their technical skills and talents to the point of qualifying for advancement, but then many hit a point where they are told they don't have "what it takes" to be effective at senior levels and that, in essence, they are not leadership material.

Feeling helplessly sidelined by the power players and structures of their organizations, women often decide that "what it takes" to get to where they want to go just might not be worth it. Many begin to settle for less, pull back on their desire for promotions, or take less senior roles and focus on other priorities.

Essentially, they abandon the goals, ambitions, and dreams that once fueled their optimism and drive.

What these women often don't yet see is that language is a significant barrier to women's advancement. It is not a barrier that many people talk about, but it *is* a barrier we, as individuals, can do something about. Language is an accessible way women can reconnect with their power and consciously create alignment between what they want to achieve and what they say.

To help more women develop a new relationship with language and their power, I designed a workshop titled *Women, Language, and Power.* The workshop has afforded me the privilege of presenting to large and diverse audiences in order to spread awareness of how women's conditioning is working against their career advancement. This book is modeled on my current *Women, Language, and Power* workshop.

In Part One of this book, I share what I have learned from researching gender bias and its effect on women's sense of power and language in professional settings. In Part Two, I provide strategies and tools I use with my clients and share with the women who attend my workshop. These resources are designed to help women focus on what they *can* control—their language and communication style—when seeking to overcome their cultural conditioning and carefully navigate gender bias in the workplace.

My goal for this book is twofold. First, I hope to convince you that language is an invaluable tool for advancement and self-actualization. As women become more skilled in using language strategically and effectively, they find they get more of what they want. Moreover, when they take the time to articulate without hesitation their own ideas, perspectives, and opinions, they themselves become more invested in and more committed to them. That commitment helps them feel empowered, confident, and even more capable of speaking to be heard.

Second, I hope to spark an important conversation among women and men. The ideas and issues I lay out in this book will lose their subversive power over women as more and more of us are aware of them.

While we need both women and men proactively working to reverse systemic gender bias and advocating for women's full equality, I have repeatedly seen women make incredible change in their own lives. Overcoming how culture constrains us is absolutely doable. It begins with discovering the ways our conditioning has fundamentally shaped—and minimized—who we are. It occurs when women rediscover and restore the categories of language and communication that our conditioning has robbed from us. It's evident when women learn to nimbly balance both stereotypically "masculine" and "feminine" styles in order to get what they want. And it has manifested when women stand fully in their power—and feel at home.

I hope this book will help you achieve just that.

A Note on Research

This book is rooted in research and my own insights gained through decades of working with women in my coaching practice. On both of these fronts, I offer two important notes.

First: The research most useful to me while developing my *Women, Language, and Power* workshop and writing this book largely relies upon white, middle-class women and men as subjects. The exclusion of people from non-white races and ethnic backgrounds, from the full spectrum of socioeconomic circumstances, from the LGBTQ community, or whose gender identification is fluid and/or nonbinary leads to results that are not truly representative.

That said, a large percentage of my female clients are women of color. The essence of their experiences, as shared with me, is captured in the studies I've referenced in this book. My experience tells me that if you were raised as a female, this book will speak to you and offer relevant and substantive solutions.

Second: In order to illustrate the insights from research and real-world experience, I share anecdotes from my clients' professional lives. To protect their privacy, I have changed names and identifying details.

A Note to Men

When I present my *Women, Language, and Power* workshop for a company, I make a point of clarifying that men are also welcome. Typically, two or three men will join the female attendees. At the end of the workshop, the men's comments are, interestingly, almost always the same. First, they say something like, "I had no idea women were in such a bind. It's so unfair they feel confined in how they speak while simultaneously knowing that both confined and expanded language pose risks to their careers." Then they say, "I can now see how I can be helpful to the women I work with." Just as the women who attended the workshop leave feeling empowered, the men's responses let me know that they do as well.

To bring about individual and collective change in how

women are treated in the workplace, they need allies. To the men reading this book, I hope to raise your awareness of the barriers women confront as they attempt to advance in their careers. This book will provide insight as to how you can support women in speaking assertively, assure them they are safe in doing so, and play your role in helping women achieve full equality in the workplace. As more women own their power and the expression of it, we are *all* more empowered as a result.

CHAPTER 1

The Cultural Dismantling of Women's Power and Voice

A few years ago, I walked into the office of a client—we'll call her Nora—for the first time. Her organization had decided to pilot a program in which "high potential" leaders were matched with an executive coach. We engaged in the usual conversation I like to have in all first meetings with new clients. She told me about her career history and how she had arrived in her new role—a story that stretched back to her upbringing in a tiny New Zealand town and included fascinating twists and turns that landed her in Northern California.

Nora had recently been tapped by a major university system to lead a newly established health policy institute. She told me she wasn't confident in her ability to make it a success. I asked her what she believed she had done to be successful up to that point in her career, thinking she could replicate it in her new position. Even though I didn't yet know much about Nora, her success seemed a foregone conclusion to me. She wouldn't have earned her multiple degrees or been entrusted with a leadership role at a high-profile institute without a track record of success. Yet this simple question stumped her. It had not occurred to Nora that she had been successful. Let me put a finer point on it: It had not occurred to Nora that she'd played the *central role* in her success, such that she could depend on herself to do it again.

I wish I could tell you that her response surprised me. But I have seen this type of self-doubt from scores of women who've come through my practice over the decades. In so many cases, it hasn't occurred to women that they—not something outside of themselves—are at the center of their success.

Sitting together in a moment of silence, Nora began to tear up. She attributed her success, she explained, to the teams on which she'd worked. She also attributed her success to chance, timing, and various other factors that were independent of her. It was not until this emotional moment that she realized she had been denying herself credit for her success.

When I ask men what has made them successful, their answers come readily and are spoken in terms of what they themselves have done to earn success. Whereas women often struggle to attribute their success to themselves, men do so easily and are not quick to consider the other people and circumstances that might have played a hand in theirs.

To a degree, other people and circumstances always *do* play a hand in our success. But it is also true that to get hired or promoted in the first place, we have to show talent, work ethic, competence, and a comfort with self-promotion, asserting our authority, being decisive, and influencing others. In the absence of these skills and attributes, no person or circumstance can achieve success for us.

To men, this is black and white, blatantly obvious. To women? It's not that simple.

When I asked Nora what her goals were in our work together, I noticed some recognizable themes. She shared that she felt like an impostor in her role as head of the institute. Being assertive made her feel controlling, and she had no interest in being a command-and-control leader. She recoiled at the notion that her ideas were superior to those of others, and she bristled at the thought of declaring them the institute's priority. But she recognized that doing so was a requirement of her new role. So she expressed a need for tools that would help her overcome her sense of being an impostor and allow her to feel confident when engaging with her peers and showing authority when leading her team. In a moment of clarity, she stated her conflict: "I just don't want to be a tall poppy." She explained that in New Zealand, "tall poppy syndrome" refers to a social practice of ridiculing or mocking people who think too highly of themselves and make themselves too visible. It was always safer, she said, to remain small.

As Nora spoke, I felt a familiar mix of compassion and astonishment. Compassion because I understand the cultural pressure for women to remain small and unimposing. Astonishment because I have worked with so many accomplished and impressive women who struggled with self-doubt despite having résumés that scream high achievement. Many of my clients, even those already at the executive level, struggle to fully see themselves as the leaders they are and embrace the power that comes with it.

Nora was no different. After earning her M.D., she completed a three-year fellowship at a high-profile public health policy program. She then took a role at a prestigious university and also joined their faculty. When I met her, she was just starting her tenure as head of the new institute. Her stellar list of achievements was still no match for her seriously stubborn impostor syndrome. So, over the next three months, we did a little digging to understand the negative self-perception standing in her way in order to replace it with a new and liberated one.

Everyone I coach has insecurity. Whether it's feeling a need to prove oneself, feeling like an impostor, being a people pleaser, struggling with a stifling case of perfectionism, or something else entirely, all people experience at least some self-doubt. Yet women have a second and deeper layer of self-doubt that comes from how our culture trains and shapes us. That conditioning, which teaches us how to achieve society's expectations of femininity, ultimately severs us from our wholeness and our power. It cripples our sense of agency, or the degree to which we believe we can make decisions and speak on behalf of the life we want and the people we want to be.

Over our entire lives, women are given the message to "rein it in." In preschool, it might be a parent insisting that it's "impolite" or "not nice" to play with a toy when someone else wants it. In grade school, it might be a teacher instructing us to sit down and wait our turn to speak. In high school, it might be peers shaming us for being "bossy" or wanting "too much" attention. In the workplace, it might be a manager demanding that we tone down our "aggressive" style as a condition of our promotion. At the leadership level, it might be a superior telling us we are "too ambitious" and outspoken about it.

From day one, women's behaviors and words are managed, policed, shamed, and corrected. This is done by moms, dads, siblings, friends, teachers, caregivers, media, and so on. The result of this conditioning tends to take a predictable form. It leaves women nervous to express their full ambitions—if we've been able to hold onto them at all through years and decades in the workforce. We end up making ourselves smaller, retreating from our power and shrinking our bodies so that we communicate in a way that is as unimposing as possible. We become apprehensive in making decisions, particularly when it might upset others. We feel hesitant to speak up, take credit, openly compete for power, and ask for what we deserve, lest we offend a delicate social and patriarchal status quo. Our conditioning also leaves us without the language to speak on behalf of our wants, needs, and ambitions.

Since the feminist revolution of the 1960s and 1970s, women have made awe-inspiring strides earning representation and careers in every industry out there. But we have not yet found equal representation in leadership roles and positions of power.

My experience coaching women reveals that impediments to advancement are not because women lack competence, ability, or potential. Nor is it due to a lack of desire. There is a much larger force at play.

The Weight of Femininity
Throughout World War II, millions of once nonworking American women were promoted en masse into the labor force. When nearly 16 million American men were deployed to serve in the war, they left between 10 and 20 percent of all job roles vacant. This dramatic reduction in the workforce would have been economically devastating had women not stepped up.

As men shipped off to battle, the U.S. government launched a massive campaign to entice women to replace them in factories, on assembly lines, and in other jobs once considered possible only for men. Inspired by Rosie the Riveter—with her comfortable and confident coveralls, unfussy bandanna, and "We can do it!" declaration—women rallied to assume men's jobs to keep the economy alive. The military recruited women with the slogan "Free a Man to Fight," which put 350,000 women in uniform to support military efforts in various capacities. They worked as noncombat pilots, truck drivers, translators, radio operators, and engineers.

As a result, an entire nation learned that women have brains and skills that made them capable of more than "women's work." Although some women had been seamstresses, teachers, or nurses, most typically performed domestic duties—cooking, cleaning, birthing, and mothering. Women's natures, it was believed, made them best suited for the role of caretaker, whereas men's natures made them best suited for the role of breadwinner.

World War II let the genie out of that bottle. When the American economy hummed along just fine—thrived, actually—with millions of women now in the workforce, it was hard to argue that *by their nature* women were less capable than men. Particularly when women were building the very machines that men were using in combat, ferrying planes and transporting cargo to army bases, and conducting simulated bombing missions in which they practiced low-flying fighter jet attacks to perfect them for combat. And let's not forget how many of these women also had children at home.

This is a very challenging genie to stuff back into the proverbial bottle. Have no doubt—men, even some women, have tried mightily since.

As men came home from the war in 1945, they wanted their

jobs back. So they took them back. Some women returned contentedly to their domestic lives, but countless others bemoaned the demotion back to "women's work." Despite what many believed was a genetic impossibility, women—just like men—had ambition. Most women, it would turn out, were unwilling to abide that lie for much longer.

Many historians look back at the America of the 1950s and see a nation with a shiny veneer and rumbling restlessness beneath the surface. Behind the white picket fences and pristine lawns of America's newly sprawling suburbs, women were growing ever resentful of their relegation to the home.

In 1957, *McCall's* magazine hired Betty Friedan to write an article on "togetherness," the domestic ideal of the happy housewife and the man who dutifully supports her and their children. For the assignment, she interviewed former classmates from Smith College fifteen years after their graduation.

As it turned out, an article on "togetherness" was not the article Friedan wrote. It was not the article she *could* write. Because what she discovered from those she interviewed was widespread malaise, disaffection, and disappointment with their lives. These women wanted careers that were available only to men. They wanted to use their brains and offer the value they knew they had in spheres beyond the domestic. Still peddling a certain image of women, *McCall's* rejected Friedan's article. But she persisted. She, too, had left behind a college degree and a onetime career to resign herself to the work of housewife and mother. She, too, wanted something else—that thing society still denied to women. Instead of abandoning the article, she expanded upon it and turned it into *The Feminine Mystique*, which was published in 1963. It was, of course, a best seller multiple times over—and a book that is considered the catalyst of the second-wave feminism that was kindling in the 1950s, caught fire in the 1960s, and continued to raise holy hell through the 1970s.

Friedan defined the feminine mystique as the cultural assumption that women would necessarily find satisfaction in marriage, sexual passivity, motherhood, and domestic work. She observed that innumerable women were unfulfilled in their small, pigeonholed lives. Yet most struggled to put their finger on what defined their unhappiness, prompting Friedan to call it "the problem that has no name."[1]

The problem was that society viewed women as a function of their supposedly uniformly docile natures. This relegated them to narrow lives that denied them the potential for the growth and self-actualization that psychologist Abraham Maslow argued was fundamental to a meaningful life. In one fell swoop, Friedan articulated what so many women felt but had struggled to say: that they, too, were capable of creating and being of value in the unlimited ways afforded to men. That they, too, possessed the thoughts, ideas, words, talents, and skills that had been considered possible only for men.

Thanks to Friedan's book, the mistaken notion that women's natures limited their possibilities took an irreparable blow. It also unleashed scores of Friedan acolytes to study sex and gender norms in order to further liberate women from their psychological chains.

One such person was Anna Fels, M.D. In her New York City psychiatric practice some decades later, Dr. Fels noticed a pattern with several of her female patients: Despite their professional dreams and successes, many women hit a point where they began to defer their ambition to that of others. Her male patients, on the other hand, showed no such pattern at any stage in their careers. Dr. Fels wanted to know why, and she set out to understand ambition and how it drives both men and women throughout their lives.

In the 2005 culmination of her research, *Necessary Dreams: Ambition in Women's Changing Live*s, Dr. Fels wrote that little girls and little boys share equally large ambitions—wanting to be an Olympic athlete, the president of the United States, a diplomat, a judge, a famous actor, a best-selling author. Dr. Fels determined that ambition consists of two specific components: 1) mastery of a specific skill set and 2) public recognition from peers in the field of that skill set and the resulting accomplishments.[2]

With this definition of ambition in mind, Dr. Fels explained that women today appear to advance through education and into early careers like men do. The work of being a strong student, applying to postsecondary school programs, and working in entry-level, middle, and even senior management jobs poses little threat to women's ambition. In other words, women do as well as men when it comes to setting out to master a specific skill set.[3]

The problem comes, Dr. Fels observed, with the second element of ambition: recognition. Pursuing recognition represented a specific and powerful "taboo" for women that could not be avoided if they wanted to progress toward actualizing their ambitions.[4] Eventually, if women want positions of increasing power and scope, they must raise their visibility within an organization. Doing so requires that they proactively advocate for recognition of their strengths and accomplishments. It is at this point in their careers that women are presented with an existential, and typically subconscious, choice: seek and receive recognition in order to continue to act on their ambitions, or abandon their ambitions in order to preserve a "feminine" identity. This is because, Dr. Fels determined, seeking recognition and maintaining a "feminine" identity are mutually exclusive. Dr. Fels concluded that the social pressure to remain "feminine" far exceeded the social permission for women to pursue recognition. Whether intuitively or from experience, her female patients grasped that if they promoted themselves at work and attempted to elevate their visibility, their "feminine" identity and reputation would be threatened.

The prohibition against openly seeking recognition is deeply ingrained. Dr. Fels quoted one sociologist who interviewed 45 senior women in management and, with amazement, noticed:

> *None of them talked of the need for visibility...No one seemed to recognize that if one is not "seen" by others as the kind of person who should have a particular job, that all the competence in the world would not get it for them. And then when the system didn't spontaneously reward these women for their work purely on its merits, they were "helplessly disappointed."[5]*

While many women prioritize preservation of feminine norms over their very real ambitions in order to avoid backlash, this is not an option without risks. If we stay silent on our achievements and strengths, we begin to hear feedback from the higher-ups like "You don't have any visibility with other senior leaders." Or "You don't speak up and articulate your position decisively and with authority." We are damned if we do and damned if we don't. No wonder so many women see it as preferable or safer simply to give up and remain in less ambitious roles or even opt out entirely.

I see this conflict repeatedly in my practice, where female clients will begin to back down from their ambitions once they have to wade into the messy territory of seeking recognition. They will say things like "I don't *have* to get the promotion in this round; clearly, it means more to him." Or "I don't want them to think I only care about the title." Or "My team did the work. I don't want it to sound like it was just me." When I hear such statements, I am reminded of Dr. Fels's poignant summation: "Women refuse to claim a central, purposeful place in their own stories, eagerly shifting the credit elsewhere and shunning recognition."

> Why does it feel like an identity crisis when we attempt to behave like the central agents of our lives?

I have coached many women who have gone to great lengths to avoid taking credit for their accomplishments or accepting recognition when it is wholly deserved. As a result, we keep ourselves separate from the full manifestation of our ambitions. If this is not a function of our gender—as it was once believed—but a reluctance to be perceived as deviating from a narrow definition of femininity, it begs the questions: How does recognition specifically threaten our sense of femininity? What is our cultural definition of femininity? When and how do we learn to conform to it? And why does it feel like an identity crisis when we attempt to behave like the central agents of our lives?

The Three Constraints on Women

Seeking answers to these questions sent me on an eye-opening journey, where I learned from an all-star lineup of brilliant feminist thinkers, gender studies experts, and language researchers. I read everything from midcentury advocates of women's liberation to modern-day inspections of the glass ceiling that remains unbreakable to so many. Each book, article, and research paper I read affirmed the experiences of the women who passed through my workshops and practice.

Drawing from the work with my clients and my own reading and research, a portrait of women's cultural conditioning began to emerge. Specifically, three predominant patterns of conditioning rose to the surface, which I call "the three constraints on women." They are the mechanisms that serve to steadily dismantle women's sense of self and mold us into something called "feminine." To get us there, they constrain our wholeness, our agency, our self-perception, our self-confidence, our ambition, our feelings, our healthy sense of entitlement, and—

We are left with only those pieces of ourselves that align to culturally sanctioned ideals of femininity.

ultimately—our language. It is not that our DNA or biology limits us. Rather, the constraints are socialization processes—so subtle we may miss them—that put women in the supporting, not central, role in our own stories.

All told, these constraints dictate the boundaries of femininity and the expectations for women's behavior from our earliest days. The three constraints—each the focus of one of the three ensuing chapters—are as follows:

Considerate: *Women are conditioned to consider others first.*
Contained: *Women are conditioned to contain their bodies and voices.*
Collaborative: *Women are conditioned to prioritize collaboration over hierarchy.*

The three constraints converge to function as a sieve; like soil through a strainer, certain parts of us are left behind. Our sense of power and central agency are separated from our sense of self. We are left with only those pieces of ourselves that align to culturally sanctioned ideals of femininity.

Constrained Language

Our words convey our thoughts and communicate who we are. If our sense of self is filtered through and winnowed down by the three constraints, our language and communication style are, as well. The constraints ultimately strip women's language repertoire of its authority and authenticity—a fact that I have witnessed time and again in my coaching practice. My work exposed me to the chasm between men's and women's language: Men use language to assert power, and women use language to convey a lack of it. My observations were validated and clarified when I was introduced to Robin Tolmach Lakoff, who published the groundbreaking essay "Language and Woman's Place" in 1973.

As a professor of linguistics at the University of California, Berkeley, Lakoff studied the differences in male and female language patterns, their roots, and their societal effects. Her research showed that language is elemental to gender inequality, in that it is both a byproduct and a reinforcer of it. She believed that society teaches women to be hesitant and lack confidence. As a result, women's language is hedged, softened, apologetic, and infused with doubt. She saw the opposite with men, who were taught by society to be domineering and in control. This allows men to use language that is infused with force, certitude, assertiveness, and sometimes aggressiveness. These qualities are emphasized through body language and a wide range of tone and volume.[6]

In Lakoff's assessment, language influences how men and women feel about themselves. She believed that language fortifies gender stereotypes and perceptions of how men and women should behave in society and relate to others. This keeps us stuck in a vicious cycle, where language limits the opportunities perceived as possible for women and the perceived possibilities for women keep language limited.

> Whereas men's language reinforces their power, women's language reinforces their lack of it.

Lakoff's work was a paradigm shift, revealing to me the inextricable link between language and power. Her insights solidified my understanding of the stark differences I saw in the way men and women communicate in business and use language to navigate their careers. Throughout my coaching career, I have seen that men are far more comfortable and confident using language to promote their work and ideas. They are better able to advocate for themselves, ask for promotions, and engage in confrontational conversations. I have also seen how women's discomfort with these kinds of conversations hold back their careers and preclude them from achieving promotions, influence, and positions of power. Women's disempowered language is the end result of a disconnection to their sense of self and power. Whereas men's language reinforces their power, women's language reinforces their lack of it.

When I began coaching, I witnessed the suffocating weight of women's cultural conditioning. And when the three constraints crystallized for me, I finally understood why women struggle to find the language to ask for what they want, articulate their ambitions, or act on their power. As we spend more time under the thumb of our conditioning and grow more disconnected from our power, we lose more and more of our language.

Therein lies the hope and opportunity. We can liberate ourselves from the three constraints and all the ways they have held us back and kept us quiet.

The Exception Proves the Rule

When I first read Lakoff's work, I saw many of my female clients represented in it. But I did not fully see myself. Every rule has its exceptions, and looking back on my childhood, I can see that I am one. Due to the idiosyncratic dynamics of my family, I was trained in a communication style different from what Lakoff described as typical for most women.

I am the youngest of four children; I have two brothers and one sister. Our home was wildly dysfunctional, with parents always at odds, arguing regularly in disturbing ways and leaving us kids to manage on our own. I was painfully shy, but I learned quickly that there was neither space nor time for shyness in my house. If you wanted to be heard or get your wants and needs met, you had to speak up and speak fast. Anytime we were all together, it was a constant fight for the floor. Once you had it, you had better make your point quickly and forcefully—if you didn't, someone else was right there to talk over you and take back the floor, and your moment was gone. It was a house where aggressively elbowing your way into position to hold the floor was not only a need but also a survival skill. At times, it was exhausting and painful. As the youngest and least-skilled speaker, I was easily talked over and dismissed.

My childhood was stressful, to be sure. The fighting in my house took its toll. But every challenge leaves its gifts if we look for them. Beneath the arguments were lessons in the art of dialogue and debate. I wasn't the only family member absorbing messages about how to speak aggressively, how to speak persuasively, and how to speak to hold someone's attention. I was just the youngest. I had the advantage of observing and learning from all of my family members who became better and better at what I will affectionately call our family "debates."

My mom, who studied acting in college, used extremely dramatic language. This gave her speaking a theatrical, performative quality. Even if what she was saying bordered on hyperbolic, her points were vivid and bold, designed to shock you into listening for what was to come. My dad was never far from a philosophy book, and I absorbed his curiosity and ability to substitute questions for statements. He taught me the powerful role that questions can play in making a point or opening up new thinking. One of my brothers would analyze an argument so incisively that he could break it down in a matter of seconds. He taught me the importance of having a logical, well-supported argument to protect yourself from attack—something I struggled with, as I preferred hand-to-hand combat over skilled intellectual debate.

My other brother was brilliant at economy of words and power of imagery. He loved using clever analogies and iconic examples to make his point. And my sister was the most measured of the four kids. She would wait for her moment and then, clearly and concisely, make a well-thought-out and formidable argument. She never lost track of her point in the emotional heat.

Despite being tense and often contentious, the communication in our house was built on the full range of language possibilities. Both the women and men in my family were encouraged, even conditioned, to speak assertively, aggressively, with drama, and without reservation. We learned to push our way to the front of the line, compete for attention, and fight it out point by point. At no point were we taught to be considerate of others, to be yielding, to defuse tension, or to soothe hurt feelings.

How my family taught me to communicate was the polar opposite of how my teachers and most peers wanted me to communicate. My family taught me that shyness gets you nowhere, so I'd long since learned to bulldoze over and disconnect from my shyness such that it—despite being my natural state—grew unfamiliar to me. Instead, my default had become an almost incessant chatter to conceal my shyness. At school, I'd talk so much that my teachers were always asking me to talk less and even made me sit for long periods of time in a coat closet. They were constantly telling me to raise my hand, let others speak, or wait my turn. In other words, they were constantly telling me to talk and behave "like a girl." Many tried to police and constrain my language and how I was using it. When they asked me to talk quietly, defer to others, and be still, it felt foreign. Because there was nothing about my homelife that was reflected in what they were asking of me. I didn't get it, and it didn't take.

This was all for better and for worse. For better, I don't have to leap miles outside of my comfort zone to assert myself with intensity and conviction. For me, these muscles are well developed. For worse, I have hurt many people in my personal and professional life with unnecessary aggression or a dismissive tone—behavioral patterns I've worked hard to overcome. Professionally, it's posed its risks, as well. Years ago, a consultant to a company I worked for told me, "You could be very influential if you were not so intense and didn't sound so angry."

In contrast to my linguistic education at home, I had an additional, very specific experience with my mother at her workplace that also left an imprint on me. Interestingly, my mom took on a different persona outside of our home. When I was in grade school, she taught a special education class at a middle school. I didn't like school (particularly the coat closet with which I'd grown so familiar), so as often as I could get away with it, I would feign being sick. This meant I had to go to work with my mom, as no one else was home to watch me during the weekday.

My mom worked out of a portable classroom trailer that was parked on the back lot of the school. Her students were assigned to her class when they were unable to keep up with their regular academic coursework. She decorated this dismal trailer with rugs, stuffed chairs, and round tables for group work. It was warm, cozy, and inviting. As she tutored her students, I would sit in the corner of the trailer in a big chair and observe. My mom spoke to her students differently from how she spoke to us in our home. While she wouldn't turn off her flair for the dramatic, she toned down the hyperbole and artfully balanced her blunt honesty with supportive language and a kinder tone.

Many of her students had been held back anywhere from one to three years. So they might have been in sixth grade but two years older than everyone in their class and still struggling to read at a fourth-grade level. These children faced numerous challenges, but my mom never doubted their potential to overcome them. She was not about to let them lose belief in themselves, either. She understood how to motivate students and was very direct in her attempts to do so. To a male student, she would say things like, "Do you want a girlfriend someday? Will you want to take her out on a date at a restaurant? If you can't read the menu, how will you ever get a girlfriend? The answer is—you won't. You don't want to be embarrassed." Then she would pivot to speaking supportively to emphasize her desire to help them. "You deserve a girlfriend," she would say. "And when you take her on a date, you're going to want to be able to read the menu. So let's do the work." Once students signaled their desire to try, my mom would sit next to them, ask them to sound out the words, and offer guidance when they got stuck.

And so began the lesson and their motivation to learn to read. When they succeeded, she'd reaffirm their efforts with kind words of encouragement. If they appeared as though they were going to give up, she'd come right back at them with a direct statement about how they simply had to figure this out and learn to read.

I would sit in awe and watch as she moved back and forth between direct and confrontational and softer, more compassionate language and tones. While it would take some decades for me to grasp the magnitude of what my mom was doing, I could see that her approach was powerful. *She* was powerful, and her students respected her and worked to meet her high expectations. She was able to make them feel whole at the exact time she was insisting they address their deficits. She confronted them while keeping their sense of empowerment intact.

My experience has made two things undeniable to me. First, women can just as easily "talk like men." Where I have been told to "tone it down," most women must be coached to "turn it up"—a practice that at first feels very unnatural to many. Second, women have to "thread a needle" when choosing their language and how they communicate it when trying to advance in their careers. We can "turn it up" only so much before we push too far, disrupt the status quo, and face backlash. Just as my mom had been with her students, women can be incredibly effective when utilizing both direct and supportive language to advance their goals.

Raucous nature aside, my upbringing made me comfortable using language in more stereotypically masculine ways, including using my whole body, more of the physical space around me, and the full range of vocal tone and volume to animate points. The pushback I got from being "too assertive" or "too aggressive," especially once I entered the working world, forced me to grow comfortable counterbalancing my communication habits with more stereotypically female ones. The net effect was that, relatively early in my career, I found myself using both stereotypically masculine and feminine ways of speaking. This left me with a far greater set of options when I chose my language and how I expressed it. It's not that I spoke like both a man and a woman. It's that I spoke like a *person*—a whole person.

Liberation Through Language

My conditioning and experience required that I bring more stereotypically feminine language into my repertoire. As I learned to soften some of the blunt force of my language, I discovered that I was more effective in my communication. While I did not need to learn to be direct, I learned how to be supportive while still being assertive and clear. In doing so, I discovered a road map for how women can leverage and exercise their power without so dramatically and rapidly upsetting social norms that they face backlash and punishment for it.

While my path to this discovery was from the opposite direction of most women's paths, I understood that any woman can change her language to change her relationship with her own power and her power dynamic with others. Any woman can rediscover the full language repertoire that has been denied her and choose language that strategically advances her goals. Any woman can learn to thread the needle and find the mix of language and effective communication style that will manifest her dreams and full ambitions.

> In changing our language to voice exactly what we want to say, in the way we want to say it, we begin to influence our thoughts about ourselves.

We often believe that our thoughts inform our language, and this is true. But I have seen it a thousand times—our language can just as easily change our thoughts. In changing our language to voice exactly what we want to say, in the way we want to say it, we begin to influence our thoughts about ourselves. We begin to roll back the cultural conditioning that has suppressed our sense of self. As we practice connecting with those stereotypically masculine language choices we've been incorrectly led to believe were antithetical to our femininity, we rediscover our natural-born power and grow more comfortable showing it to ourselves and others. We view ourselves as larger and more multifaceted than we have before. We begin to experience our wholeness and learn how to live within it.

From our wholeness, women are unstoppable.

After I began my work with Nora, she made consistent and courageous efforts to change her language and how she used it, and she quickly changed herself. She spent more time speaking in an honest, direct, and unfiltered way. Within a few months, she had developed a stronger presence and greater confidence as a woman and a leader.

We first worked on her language to communicate and enforce clear boundaries and expectations at work. Because she believed she had to put everyone else first, she thought she had to accommodate all requests. This created a situation where she was so consumed by other people's low-priority requests that she had no time to focus on her ideas for the institute. For example, Nora observed that a lax and unclear work-from-home policy was disrupting productivity. Yet people had expressed the desire for this flexibility, so she had been hesitant to deny it. We worked on using language that was direct and unapologetic, such as "Our productivity has declined since we instituted a work-from-home option. As of September 15, I will be changing the policy for working at home. Until further notice, we will all work in the office. If there are special circumstances that may require accommodation, I will handle each decision on a case-by-case basis."

From there, we had to liberate her small sense of self—that part of her that was terrified of being perceived as a tall poppy. In our conversations about what it means not just to have the title of a leader but also to *act* like a leader, it hit Nora: Leaders *are* tall poppies! In effect, her fear of being cut down to size shaped her leadership philosophy, and she and her team were paying dearly for it. When Nora reframed her perception of leaders as tall poppies, she finally grasped that her team *wanted* her to be a leader and *needed* her vision and guidance. Nora's vision was clear to her, so we worked on language to share it with others and, in no uncertain terms, communicate it as the vision of the institute. We chose strong language, like "I am sharing with you my vision and intentions for the institute" as opposed to "These are some thoughts for the institute." We chose language that projected confidence, such as "I know we can achieve the goals laid out in my vision" rather than "I hope we will get there with our hard work."

Lastly, we worked on language that would allow Nora to step into the mindset and power of a leader—to the benefit of herself, her team, and the organization. This required that she unapologetically delegate smaller priorities and tasks to free up her time to build the institute, socialize her vision, create alignment across the organization for her vision, and recruit partners. We drafted language like this: "Although I have greatly benefited from being a part of this task force, I will no longer be able to attend meetings as of October 1. My new role will require a substantial amount of my time to establish the institute. I look forward to updates on your activities and offering support in a new capacity."

Nora came to see that she was too valuable and her role too big for less crucial activities. She came to understand that, in her new role, she was too powerful to let herself remain bogged down by her cultural conditioning. Doing so would undermine not only her success but also the institute's.

We can view Nora's story in one of two ways. We can be baffled by how a woman so credentialed and accomplished could lack confidence and be plagued by impostor syndrome at this stage in her career. Or we can consider how the messages she absorbed from society served to keep her small and separate from her power. We can consider all of the cultural training she received—about not standing out, not speaking up for her ideas, and not thinking she was all that smart. We can consider all the ways people made her believe her role is to put others first and speak in a way that makes everyone feel comfortable and included. And, despite all this cultural conditioning, we can marvel at what she still managed to achieve.

I see it the second way. What we women achieve, in spite of all the cultural forces working against us, is nothing short of phenomenal. Yet seeing this view requires that we understand the potent effect of our cultural conditioning and the three constraints: Considerate, Contained, and Collaborative. Our cultural constraints are real, powerful, and oppressive. But they are a lie. You are not genetically destined to live according to the three constraints. In absorbing this lie, we accept the gendered assumptions that rob us of our central agency and full ambition.

In absorbing this lie, we have denied our wholeness.

This is not a reason to despair. Paradoxically, women have developed certain superpowers—namely, a categorical gift for demonstrating compassion, practicing inclusion, building consensus, and cultivating a collective vision. The world needs our superpowers. But it needs our wholeness more.

Our language holds the key.

Talking Our Way to the Top

In the ensuing chapters, I show you how each of the three constraints limits women's sense of self and potential for advancement. I give examples of how we as children absorb the constraints as a fact of our gender and how they inhibit our options when we carry them over into our adult lives. I demonstrate empirically that we *all* have the same wherewithal, capacity, and know-how to communicate assertively, clearly, powerfully, and shrewdly in order to advance our careers and achieve our dreams.

I also explain how this advancement has been denied to us. We are not denied advancement because of something inherent in our natures or because it's not a "woman's place." It is because, for centuries, society has systematically trained us to believe that women are not wired to use language that is direct, forceful, authoritative, or animated. In moments when we must speak strongly, we have been led to believe that we must borrow a style of communication from somewhere outside of us and then quickly return it to its place before it becomes toxic.

My goal in writing this book is to offer you language and communication choices from a full repertoire so that you can begin to create a different power dynamic—with yourself and with others. I will show you how to integrate language and communication styles that will advance y*our* purpose, *your* ambitions, and *your* power. Your professional aspirations will thank you. They demand your advocacy and voice today—because time has a way of chipping away at those dreams if we don't intervene on their behalf and step into the power they require of us.

Just as the women of Friedan's era struggled to articulate their malaise and dissatisfaction with small, domestic lives, today we struggle to articulate our ambition and power. As was the case in the 1950s, the language doesn't yet feel comfortable or socially acceptable to us. Once the women of Friedan's era were able to pinpoint and articulate their desire for work beyond the domestic sphere in order to self-actualize and build a meaningful life, they had a defined problem and could then fashion a targeted solution.

Today, once we recognize the problem of how the three constraints erode our sense of wholeness and thereby restrict our power and our language, we can solve it. We can quite literally talk ourselves out of it and talk our way to the top.

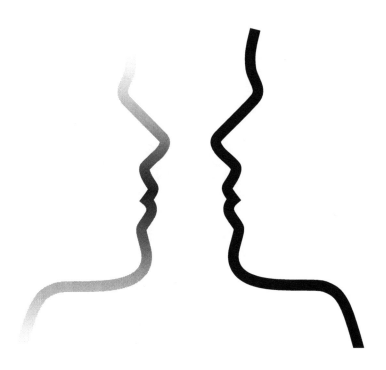

CHAPTER 2

Considerate

How Women Are Conditioned
to Consider Others First

Like many of my clients, Grace was hoping to advance her career. Her manager had told her that a promotion to vice president was within reach in the coming year, but she had to improve in asserting her ideas and increasing her visibility among leadership. In one of our sessions, she shared a recent experience she'd had in a meeting that all of the VPs attended. Since it was her meeting to lead and facilitate, it was a moment for her to shine in front of people who were key stakeholders and whose impressions of her mattered.

She'd asked her direct report to take meeting notes. But once in the meeting, she noticed there was no paper, pen, or open laptop in front of him. Here she was, trying to lead this meeting in front of potential peers, and she was increasingly frustrated and distracted by this direct report's failure to do his job. To make matters worse, he was enjoying chatting with some of the VPs. Despite her irritation, she made the choice to take the notes herself, compromising her ability to focus on the discussion.

In our session, I asked Grace why she didn't prompt him to carry out his responsibility then and there. She said, "I didn't want to interrupt him and humiliate him in front of all the VPs."

I suggested there was a different way to look at the situation. Given that she wanted to be a VP, it was humiliating for *her* to be doing administrative tasks in front of a group of senior people who need to view her as a peer. Her focus should have been on what she was trying to accomplish, not on what her direct report might have wanted in that important meeting.

While the details change, I hear this type of story often in my practice—the story of professional women deferring their needs and priorities out of consideration for someone else's feelings. In an effort to protect and prioritize others' feelings, women will literally hurt their own careers. Most women, in my experience, do not see it this way. They also do not see any other options. Consciously or not, many women have accepted as an unavoidable reality that prioritizing their own needs and ambitions will make others uncomfortable. They will go to great lengths to defer to others in corporate settings. We have the power to change this. But first we must identify what's behind this reflex to consider other people's comfort before something as significant as our own objectives, goals, and achievements.

> In an effort to protect and prioritize others' feelings, women will literally hurt their own careers.

In 2013, Herminia Ibarra, Robin J. Ely, and Deborah M. Kolb—all professors at different business schools who study gender and leadership—published "Women Rising: The Unseen Barriers" in the *Harvard Business Review*. The authors had seen many CEOs prioritize gender diversity and create pipelines to increase the share of women in leadership roles, only to become disappointed to realize their efforts had made little difference. By and large, few women were rising to the top.

Subtle gender bias remains entrenched in society and prohibits women in organizations from seeing themselves as leaders and acting like leaders, according to Ibarra, Ely, and Kolb.[1] Even a well-designed mentor or training program may not promote women to leadership levels if they ultimately do not experience a shift in mindset and identity to that of a leader. They will at some point either find themselves stuck while others are promoted over them—or some will opt out of the pursuit of advancement or careers entirely.

Ibarra et al. blame "second-generation gender biases" for women's struggle to develop the identity of a leader. First-generation gender bias amounted to the outright exclusion of women in most industries. Now women are part of corporate culture, but they remain underrepresented in leadership roles due to more subtle "unseen barriers." The authors identify four second-generation biases:

1) **A dearth of role models for women at leadership levels.** Because there are few aspirational career women serving as role models, there are fewer opportunities for young women to observe female leadership styles and experiment with them on their own.

2) **Gendered career paths and gendered work.** Many companies have promotion paths that were designed to match men's lives (e.g., the need to travel or complete a job rotation program that requires moving around to various cities). Companies also undervalue "behind-the-scenes" work, such as team building or avoiding crises, which is typically done by women.

3) **Lack of access to networks and sponsors.** Since there are so few female leaders, female workers must rely on male leaders for many networking opportunities. But men tend to network primarily with men, leaving female workers a small networking pool.

4) **Double binds.** The double bind that professional women find themselves in is that the skills prized and required for leaders are the very skills that society has discouraged women from developing and applying. They are the skills that, if women were supported in developing and using, would facilitate their adoption of an identity as leaders. This is the unseen barrier that interests me most because it is the one I observe most often as the driving force behind women's underrepresentation in leadership and the three other barriers.[2]

This double bind is the "damned if we do, damned if we don't" predicament that psychiatrist Anna Fels discovered when researching ambition. Recall from Chapter 1 that Dr. Fels noticed a pattern with her female patients. Eventually, many successful women hit a point in their careers where their ambition begins to be "too much," in that it makes others uncomfortable and starts to create problems. Dr. Fels diagnosed this as the point where women must choose either to preserve their sense of feminine identity at the expense of acting on their ambition or continue to act on their ambition at the expense of their feminine identity. Dr. Fels also noticed that what's at stake in this choice—the feminine identity—is largely subconscious.

What are these notions of femininity that are so strong they can cause women to put others in front of their own ambitions and leadership potential? And apparently drive major life decisions without our conscious awareness? Where do they come from?

Conditioned to Be Considerate

Nearly a half century ago, back in 1974, an American psychologist and onetime active leader in the women's liberation movement, Sandra Bem, sought empirical evidence that communication and behavior are not the domain of one's biological sex but rather a collection of characteristics. While these characteristics were thought to be genetically feminine, genetically masculine, or neutral, Bem theorized that each could be exhibited by anyone despite his or her chromosomes.

In order to test her theory, Bem created the Bem Sex-Role Inventory, or BSRI. She began by listing 200 personality characteristics that were desirable and either typically associated with women or typically associated with men. She also compiled a list of 200 characteristics typically considered to be gender-neutral, half of which were viewed as desirable and half of which were not. Bem then distributed this list of 400 characteristics to 100 undergraduate students at Stanford University. Each characteristic was judged on a scale from one to seven, where one meant "not at all desirable" and seven meant "extremely desirable." Fifty of the students were asked to judge all characteristics in terms of their desirability for women, and the other 50 were asked to judge them in terms of their desirability for men.

Based on the students' responses, Bem compiled an ultimate

list of the 60 characteristics of the BSRI (see Figure 1). On the "feminine scale", are the twenty characteristics deemed most desirable for women, and on the "masculine scale" are the twenty characteristics deemed most desirable for men. Bem also added the "social desirability scale," which included twenty characteristics that are judged as no more or less desirable for men or women. Ten of them are considered positive, and ten are considered negative.

Bem's intention for the BSRI was for it to be used as a research tool to "assess the extent to which the culture's definitions of desirable female and male attributes are reflected in an individual's self-description."[3] In fact, the BSRI is one of the most widely used tools to study gender roles to this day. Those who take the BSRI rank themselves along all 60 characteristics on a seven-point scale, where one means a respondent's identification with a characteristic is "never or almost never true," and seven means "always or almost always true."

Well into the 21st century, it can be tempting to look at this list and dismiss it as outdated, a cultural relic that we have—thank goodness—moved past. After all, what self-serious woman acts "childlike" or "gullible" in order to be desired? The implication that such characteristics are intrinsically feminine and a requirement of a woman's desirability is grotesque and easy to write off as culturally obsolete. In certain ways, it *is* obsolete. In a 1992 study, survey respondents judged only one of all 60 BSRI characteristics as stereotypically feminine and only one as stereotypically masculine: "feminine" and "masculine," respectively.[4] Eighteen years after the BSRI's creation, it appeared we had experienced certain reformed cultural judgments around gender norms. However, evidence suggests that these reformed judgments have made only a surface-level impact on social norms.

Bem Sex-Role Inventory (BSRI)

Feminine Scale	Masculine Scale	Social Desirability Scale
yielding	self-reliant	helpful
cheerful	defends own beliefs	moody
shy	independent	conscientious
affectionate	athletic	theatrical
flatterable	assertive	happy
loyal	strong personality	unpredictable
feminine	forceful	reliable
sympathetic	analytical	jealous
sensitive to others' needs	leadership ability	truthful
understanding	willing to take risks	secretive
compassionate	makes decisions easily	sincere
eager to soothe hurt feelings	self-sufficient	conceited
soft spoken	dominant	likable
warm	masculine	solemn
tender	willing to take a stand	friendly
gullible	aggressive	inefficient
childlike	acts as a leader	adaptable
does not use harsh language	individualistic	unsystematic
loves children	competitive	tactful
gentle	ambitious	conventional

Figure 1

The Systematic Suppression of a Girl's Sense of Self

In 2006, when one of my two daughters, Jessica, was thirteen, she was invited to a bar mitzvah for a boy in her class. The party after the ceremony was going to be at a "totally cool" club in San Francisco, and the "perfect" dress was a must. Much care and thought went into her appearance because—as I learned that evening—Jess had a crush on this boy. After returning home from the party, she rushed through the front door, said two sentences about how incredible the evening was, and then got very serious.

"Mom, I don't know if he likes me," she said.

Somewhat surprised to hear this statement from my typically confident daughter, I gently asked, "What makes you think he doesn't like you, Jess?"

"What if I'm too much for him?" she asked with concern.

Hearing her say these words shocked me. I knew she was getting at something profoundly disturbing. It took me a minute to realize what it was. Hundreds of times, I'd heard female clients speak this same sentiment, worried that they would come off as "too aggressive," "too bossy," or just "too much" of anything they've discerned could offend others or disrupt a certain social balance. At the young age of thirteen, my daughter had already detected the risks and potential consequences. Being "too much" of some ill-defined characteristics could impact her likability and, more importantly, her desirability to boys.

Conversations with my daughters about how to assert themselves, speak up for themselves, and defend themselves are not uncommon in our household. Even when they were in middle school, they had grown skilled and comfortable with asserting themselves effectively with peers. But I underestimated their perceptions of how such behaviors would impact their interactions with boys. I had failed to grasp that without addressing this topic head-on, they too would begin to suppress aspects of themselves to avoid offending the opposite sex.

This systematic dismantling of girls' self-concept in order to fit a socially desirable mold is the phenomenon Rachel Simmons explores in her 2009 book, *The Curse of the Good Girl: Raising Authentic Girls With Courage and Confidence.* "Our culture is teaching girls to embrace a version of selfhood that sharply curtails their power and potential," Simmons writes. "In particular, the pressure to be 'Good'—unerringly nice, polite, modest, and selfless—diminishes girls' authenticity and personal authority."[5] She goes on to make the case that not only are girls still taught to be the quintessential "Good Girl," but they are also given impossible and conflicting standards that stymie their potential and power.

Simmons is a cofounder of Girls Leadership, a nonprofit institute that designs middle school and high school curricula to "teach girls to exercise the power of their voice" and to develop leadership and career-relevant abilities, such as negotiation, self-advocacy, and compromise. Over the years, Simmons has gathered responses from girls who've attended the institute as to

> At the young age of thirteen, my daughter had already detected the risks and potential consequences. Being "too much" of some ill-defined characteristics could impact her likability and, more importantly, her desirability to boys.

what they believe a "Good Girl" looks and acts like. Typical responses include *quiet, perfect, no opinions on things, follower, has to do everything right, polite, enthusiastic, generous, kind, intelligent, athletic, listens, honest, respectful, organized, flirtatious, speaks well, follows the rules, doesn't get mad, average, Barbie, confident, façade never cracks,* and *people pleaser.* On the other hand, they often view "Bad Girls" as *arguing, rule breaker, foul mouthed, doesn't care what people think, fights, tough attitude, proud, loud, selfish, speaks her mind, obnoxious, center of attention, rebel,* and *slut*.[6]

A comparison of the 2009 "Good Girl list" to the 1974 BSRI feminine scale reveals preserved feminine stereotypes and some small indications of progress. Nearly all of the BSRI feminine scale characteristics define femininity in terms of how women must behave relative to others; namely, it is desirable for women to consider the needs and feelings of others before their own. Thirty-five years later, Simmons' Good Girl list captured this same conception of female existence in childhood (e.g., polite, generous, kind, pleasing), and it layers it with perfectionism. The list suggests progress in that girls today are internalizing messages that they, too, are capable of intelligence and athleticism. But these messages are muddied by the concurrent expectation that intelligent and athletic girls must also be Barbie-like without opinions. According to Simmons, this leaves girls in a bind as they try to navigate just how much of something they can be before they become too much of it and are punished or have to back off. Sound familiar?

If we juxtapose Simmons's "Bad Girl list" against the BSRI masculine scale, we see that double bind. Many of the Bad Girl items are similar to the BSRI masculine scale characteristics. Women who defend their own beliefs or are willing to take a stand (BSRI masculine scale) are often seen as argumentative or possessing a tough attitude (Bad Girl list). Women who are assertive and aggressive (BSRI masculine scale) are called loud or obnoxious (Bad Girl list). Women who take risks (BSRI masculine scale) are called rule breakers or rebels (Bad Girl list). Women who act as leaders (BSRI masculine scale) are seen as needing to be the center of attention (Bad Girl list).

In terms of how girls are conditioned to behave, little has changed in the modern era, and girls remain hesitant to demonstrate leadership. For example, a 2008 report from the Girl Scouts Research Institute found that girls aged eight to seventeen believed that taking leadership positions would elicit negative reactions from peers. They also worried they would be called "bossy," which is arguably the adolescent version of "bitchy."[7] Simmons references different research that found girls are much less likely than boys to want to be in charge of others.[8]

> **Without sufficient counter-messaging, little girls will be conditioned from an early age to deny their own goals and dreams in deference to others' needs.**

Simmons points out that the "girl power" campaigns that abound today have made only a surface-level impact on girls' sense of self. While their college applications paint a picture of teenage girls with giant aspirations, if young women are inhibited by the fear of being "too much," the full realization of their aspirations will fall short. The unseen barriers can deform ambition and create an identity crisis when women deviate from feminine norms. Without sufficient counter-messaging, little girls will be conditioned from an early age to deny their own goals and dreams in deference to others' needs. They will suppress natural parts of themselves for the sake of making others comfortable. So potent and internalized are these messages that even by middle school, girls are already grasping that to be a leader is to act against how society prefers they behave.

Being Considerate and Being a Leader: Agendas at Odds

The research holds an unambiguous message. In terms of behavioral expectations, leadership is the exclusive domain of men. If one is to be a leader, one must demonstrate *leadership ability* and a comfort with *acting as a leader*, for starters. One must be willing to *defend one's beliefs*, *take a stand*, and *take risks*. One must be *ambitious*, be *forceful* at times, and *make decisions easily*. Obviously, a leader must be *assertive* and sometimes *aggressive* or *dominant*, particularly when it comes to the *competitive* nature of business. In other words, one must exhibit the BSRI characteristics that are desirable only for men.

> The effect is a life lived through the lens of others and how we might, at any given time, make them feel.

On the other end, the BSRI feminine characteristics create a picture of someone who is meant to behave in ways that are in direct opposition to behaving like a leader. What is leaderly about being *yielding*, *shy*, or *eager to soothe hurt feelings*? How can one be decisive when she must also be *warm*, *tender*, *gentle*, and *loyal*? How can one successfully manage the typical highs and lows of leading people and organizations if she must remain *cheerful* and *soft-spoken* and avoid *harsh language*?

In terms of gender norms, the feminine experience is defined by its relativity to others. To be feminine is to be considerate of everyone outside of yourself. It is to pacify and comfort others. The effect is a life lived through the lens of others and how we might, at any given time, make them feel.

"Others" show up nowhere—explicitly or implicitly—in the BSRI masculine scale. To be masculine is to be *self-reliant*, *self-sufficient*, and *individualistic*. Men are free to act in their own self-interests and on their own ambitions without experiencing a crisis of masculinity or a departure from a culturally safe identity. This does cut both ways, as men suffer if they exhibit many of the characteristics on the feminine scale. But when it comes to career advancement, men live in a world that remains rigged in their favor.

Today, it is acceptable for women to delay marriage and having children in order to establish a career. Sometimes we are even applauded for it. But make no mistake: We are still expected to hold others at the center of our experience. We can maintain a culturally defined "feminine" existence and advance a career simultaneously for only so long. Eventually, the two competing and diametrically opposed agendas will clash.

The fact that women are willing to defer their ambitions and find themselves unable to advance to senior levels offers proof that the conceptions of femininity and leadership captured in the BSRI run deep. As a matter of conditioning, these conceptions remain largely intact today, as evidenced by Simmons's Good Girl and Bad Girl lists. While we've seen some positive changes in how we perceive the masculine and feminine, these changes have yet to fully penetrate the corporate world. Furthermore, when women *do* behave like leaders, they pay a price for it.

The Likability of Female Leaders

A while back, a woman was referred to me at the request of her manager. While I hadn't met this woman, her reputation preceded her. Michelle was a VP known for her exceptional results. She was a rising star in the sales world—so much so that, frankly, I was a little surprised she wanted coaching.

In our first meeting, Michelle expressed frustration. Unlike Nora, she could identify her strengths and articulate what she had done to lead her team toward enormous sales growth. The problem? Her manager had suggested that, if she wanted a promotion to senior vice president, she would have to "change" her style and her relationship with her team. I came to find out that "change" meant something along the lines of "warm up" her interactions. I shared her frustration—would this ever have been a promotion requirement for a man?

In essence, Michelle's superior was telling her that she was acting "too masculine" for a woman; but of course, he didn't see it this way. He likely did not know to see it this way. Because to see it this way would first require an awareness of how deeply embedded our cultural definitions of femininity and masculinity are, particularly as related to leadership. And it would require an awareness of how our culture dings women who are perceived as "acting masculine" when they act like leaders. This superior, and apparently others on Michelle's team, wanted her to behave in ways that felt more feminine. Her deviation from long-held gender expectations had made some on her team uncomfortable.

To inform our coaching work, I interviewed all the members of Michelle's team to gauge their perceptions of her. I spoke with some who appreciated her "cut to the chase" approach and the way she focused on providing them the resources they needed in order to be successful. But then there were others who took serious issue with her "lack of warmth." They wanted a "personal" relationship with her. Specifically, one of her team members lamented that, in their Monday morning meetings, Michelle didn't ask them personal questions or reveal personal information about her life outside the office. Never mind that her leadership and unfaltering support of their performance had enabled them *all* to be successful and highly effective in the organization. Apparently, this was not enough to warrant a promotion.

I would come to learn that Michelle keeps firm and clear boundaries between the professional and the personal. You will never hear her discussing with her colleagues the person she is dating or asking them about their personal lives. Despite the implications of certain team members wanting this kind of interaction with her, there was nothing wrong about her boundaries, and I was not going to ask her to budge on something so important to her. But she had been given the condition of changing her style as a criterion for a promotion, so we devised a plan that included measures such as occasional team dinners and check-ins—small activities that nurtured team relationships without Michelle having to become more stereotypically "feminine" and maternal. In strategy, it was an approach I use often with women who are trying to straddle the line between appearing both like a leader and sufficiently "feminine" without sacrificing either.

This predicament—that female leaders have to somehow be both effective and "feminine"—is what Alicia Menendez refers to as "the likability trap." In her book of the same name, Menendez—a journalist and MSNBC anchor—explores the conundrum women face around the issue of likability. In short, strong female leaders are seen as cold, and warm female leaders are seen as weak. Menendez offers a different view of the same fundamental issue that Dr. Fels examined in her book, *Necessary Dreams*. Where Dr. Fels looked at this trap through the lens of ambition, Menendez looked at it through the lens of likability.

According to Menendez, women have become preoccupied with needing to be liked and put others at ease.[9] Given our early and constant conditioning to put others first, this should come as no surprise. It should also come as no surprise that women are expected to be likable in order to advance in their careers. But this only works up to a point.

In general, women tend to advance up to managerial positions, where they must team-build, nurture talent, and foster collaboration. They must be understanding and sensitive to the needs of the team in order to cultivate a supportive environment and healthy dynamics. In other words, managers must be "other-focused." There's a reason the research shows women are better managers than men: Being other-focused is the air we breathe.[10]

Eventually, though, women hit a wall, or a glass ceiling. They will find themselves stalling in their advancement, particularly when their eyes are on leadership roles. It is at this point that women begin hearing feedback such as "You haven't found your voice." "You don't speak up enough." "You don't assert your ideas aggressively." "You aren't decisive enough." "You let others talk over you." "You lack executive presence." In order to address such feedback, women have to do the very thing they have always been told *not* to do: deprioritize consideration of all others and put themselves and their ambition first.

Simply put, the likability trap looks like this: First, women must be liked in order to achieve early career success and steadily climb the corporate ladder. Then, once we begin to approach leadership levels, we are in effect told we are "too likable" to be viewed as leaders. Finally, when we attempt to behave like leaders, we are told we have a "likability issue." So, we are trapped in the prison of likability with which only women must contend.

No wonder so many women who confront this dilemma choose to downgrade their ambitions, let go of big dreams, or just opt out. No wonder so many women choose to preserve their culturally sanctioned sense of femininity in order to remain liked—the need to be liked is so deeply ingrained in our experience that separating from it can feel like an identity crisis. And no wonder so many women internalize the lessons learned from observing women who do persist, who do follow their ambitions, and who do land leadership roles—in many cases, they are punished for it.

In a 2004 paper, "Penalties for Success: Reactions to Women Who Succeed at Male Gender-Typed Tasks," its authors—Madeline Heilman, Aaron Wallen, Daniella Fuchs, and Melinda Tamkins, all professors from New York University and Columbia University—tested and confirmed their hypothesis that women suffer for their success. When women unambiguously and objectively achieve a successful performance outcome at levels typically considered the domain of men (for example, senior leadership and the C-suite), they are less liked and more likely to be personally denigrated (e.g., called a bitch, selfish, argumentative, or difficult). And they are more likely to have their femininity or sexuality impugned (e.g., called a ballbuster, lesbian, or man-hater). This can have a direct impact on their continued advancement or potential for reward and recognition in the organization.[11]

When women are penalized for success, the hypocrisy and willful blindness to those second-generation biases is staggering.

As the paper's authors stated: "…although there is a good fit between what the woman is perceived to be like and what the job is thought to entail, there is a bad fit between what the woman is perceived to be like and the conception of what she should be like."[12]

When it comes to advancing careers and climbing the ranks of leadership, what women "should" be like is more important than how women actually are.

Defer, Deny, and Demean: How Being Considerate Impacts Our Careers

When Elisa started her job as the senior director of learning and organizational development at a lifestyle company, it had neither official learning programs nor an appreciation for the role that such programs could play in the company's growth. Elisa changed all of that. Under her direction, the company designed and implemented learning initiatives that solved real company problems through management, leadership, and coaching programs. She is recognized throughout the organization as having single-handedly built a thriving learning culture that has positively impacted employee engagement and the bottom-line health and revenue of the organization.

Elisa wanted—and deserved—to be promoted to vice president. For two years, she had raised the issue with her manager. For two years, he promised her a promotion—at some unnamed future point in time. He would repeatedly say things like "Now's not a good time" or "Let me consult the leadership team." Never did he provide constructive feedback as to why her promotion was delayed yet again—feedback that might have empowered

Elisa. Meanwhile, she watched several peers advance in different areas of the organization.

In one of our coaching sessions, I asked Elisa why she did not press her manager to provide the specific reasons for the delayed promotion or a decision by an identified date. She recoiled at the thought.

"I don't want him to think I only care about the salary and not the work," she said. "And I don't want to appear unreasonable or create a situation where, if the promotion is denied, I have to leave the company."

In avoiding asking assertive questions or making direct requests of her manager, Elisa was actually avoiding potential backlash for deviating from feminine expectations. Per the findings of psychologist and professor Corinne Moss-Racusin, such avoidance from women is common. When she was a Ph.D. candidate, Moss-Racusin focused her dissertation on research into her hypothesized backlash avoidance model (BAM). Moss-Racusin found that women intuitively grasp the threat of reprisal for promoting themselves because they understand that doing so requires that they behave "like men."[13] Fear of backlash serves to push many women to self-promote within the BAM, meaning that they will talk themselves out of the idea that they are entitled to self-promote in the first place in order to avoid backlash. As a result, when it's time to self-promote, their language is hedged and unfocused. Not surprisingly, this makes women less successful at self-promoting compared to men, who are unencumbered by backlash fears.

Moss-Racusin's research affirms what I see in my practice. Women are afraid to promote themselves and their accomplishments because they have either experienced backlash personally or seen other women pay a price—materially and/or in reputation. Yet self-promotion and assuring our visibility within an organization are inevitable requirements of advancement. So women find themselves in this double bind they did not create but are responsible for navigating if they want to advance.

While the specifics change, the contours of women's reticence to self-promote with conviction in requests for more pay, scope, or power or to promote their ideas to increase visibility in the company remain the same. How women demonstrate their reticence to self-promote falls into one of three categories: defer, deny, or demean. I call them "the three Ds." In order to avoid backlash to self-promotion of any kind, women will:

Defer

Defer to others' ambitions: "I don't think about what I want. When new executives come in and claim the scope of their work, I just carve out a place for myself around it." If we are in competition with others for the same resources or opportunities (e.g., pay, budget, projects, promotions), we tend to defer and make it easier for others to win or gain.

Defer to others' ideas: "It's too risky to speak up and disagree. I just go along to make it easier." If we voice our ideas at all, we will often defer to those of others, especially if our ideas are in competition with them. We will often back down from fighting for our ideas because we know the potential costs are real.

Defer to others' talking: "I am so tired of trying to fight off the people who interrupt and dismiss me! Sometimes it's easier just to let it happen." When attempting to make our voices heard, we are often talked over or ignored. In many cases, we will grow quiet, let others talk, and won't demand that we finish or add to our point. But we resent it.

Defer our ambitions and opt out of careers: "I am tired of fighting this fight. I don't want to keep pushing for what I want or deserve." When our ambition leads us to leadership opportunities and we begin receiving messages that we are doing damage to our likability, many of us will let go of our leadership aspirations and remain in our current positions indefinitely. Some women will leave organizations and even careers behind; this is more likely when they are also facing pressures to have or tend to children.

Deny

Deny self-promotion: "I don't want to be seen as selfish or that I only care about the title or the salary." The more we advance, the more we must promote our achievements and skills. The more we self-promote, the more likely we are to receive messages that our behavior is too assertive, too aggressive, or arrogant, causing us to back off from such actions and begin missing opportunities.

Deny recognition: "I don't like to be in the spotlight. I don't need it. My work speaks for itself." As we succeed, we are likely to hear praise or be given opportunities to showcase our successes and achievements. When we do, we are more likely to garner negative attention from both women and men. So we begin to shy from praise, pass on opportunities to be in the spotlight, minimize our accomplishments, and give credit for our successes to others.

Demean

Demean ourselves by avoiding conflict to protect others' feelings: "I want to avoid confrontation. I don't want to create or work in a confrontational environment. It is just not worth it." When we allow others to take advantage of us or treat us with disregard or disrespect, we demean ourselves. When we do not push back on others in order to protect their feelings, we are demeaned. We demean our rightful authority and the baseline respect to which we are entitled.

Demean ourselves by allowing others to take credit for our contributions or work product: "It doesn't matter if I get the credit. The work got done, and the outcome was good." As we accomplish more, people will try to take credit for our successes or take full credit for teamwork for which our contributions were integral. In allowing this to happen unchallenged, we demean **ourselves and our value.**

Demean ourselves by not asking for more: "I could kick myself for not having asked for more, but it seemed like I was already asking for too much. Do you think it was too much?" Research shows that, compared to men, women expect and ask for less—be it for scope, power, responsibility, or compensation. In doing so, we demean our value, our contributions, and our potential.

Demean ourselves by settling for less: "I know I deserve more, and I have waited so long. But I don't want to look ungrateful." In not asking decisively and forcefully for what we deserve, we demean our value, our ambitions, and our dreams.

Reversing and Rejecting the Three Ds

In my experience, women often default to the three Ds. Because we've been trained to do so. For decades, we can defer, deny, and demean ourselves without awareness of what we're doing or noticing the subtle ways it harms us. It is not until we want more responsibility, a higher salary, a promotion, or a leadership role that we confront a painful, angering, and frustrating truth: that our behavior is reaffirming the problem we did not create. It is painful to realize how many times we have lost out on advancement or more pay because of our discomfort with making others uncomfortable or fear of backlash. It is angering to see clearly the double bind we are in—that if we attempt to stop deferring, denying, or demeaning ourselves in favor of our ambitions, we risk paying

> It is frustrating to accept that in order to achieve our goals, we have to behave in ways that run counter to all of our cultural conditioning.

a price. It is frustrating to accept that in order to achieve our goals, we have to behave in ways that run counter to all of our cultural conditioning.

Many women with whom I work tell me they resent the need to develop a more defiant mindset, one that includes a resolve to take action when others demand we consider their feelings over ours. They resent that they have to speak in a way that at first feels aggressive, selfish, and uncomfortable. They resent that they must use language in ways that might make others feel awkward, even when that language communicates reasonable and justified requests.

I always remind them that their anger and resentment are justified. Not only does this unseen barrier, this double bind, exist; it is also not of our creation, yet it becomes our problem to solve. If that doesn't warrant earned and defensible anger, I don't know what does. To make matters worse, we have been told for so long that anger is unfeminine. We will dive into the conditioned containment of our so-called "negative" emotions in the next chapter and in Chapter 7. For now, I will share that in my practice I often have to encourage women to feel their anger and promise them they are safe doing so in my presence. I reassure them that in being angry, they will not sacrifice their femininity. Nor will it make them a "bad person," which is often what women fear.

Getting in touch with our anger is a necessary part of unwinding years of conditioning. When we recognize our anger for what it is—a natural reaction that we can move past only by moving through—it can be converted into fuel to do the uncomfortable thing and get the reward. In fact, getting in touch with anger is often the thing that motivates many of my clients to take action.

That's exactly what Elisa did. Elisa let herself feel her anger and resentment toward her manager for keeping her in a holding pattern for *two years*. We talked about why specifically she was so angry so that she could acknowledge her feelings and take them seriously. We also discussed that, if she were to get the promotion, she would have to engage in uncomfortable and confrontational conversations to establish a different power dynamic. In advocating for herself in this instance, she would grow better prepared to do the same in all areas of her professional life.

With Elisa's anger now channeled into the energy needed to

assert herself, we wrote a script for a meeting with her manager. The script was designed to cover four points:

1) Her specific accomplishments, including programs created, people trained, and organizational impacts

2) A request to be given feedback on any specific areas that were hindering her promotion

3) A request for a specified date by which she would have a formal answer about her promotion

4) Her assumption that if, by the agreed-upon date her manager told her, he was still waiting for any reason, she would consider this a denial of her promotion

Elisa went into the meeting with her manager with a new conviction: She believed herself to be reasonable in her requests, entitled to them, and well within her right to push for the outcome she wanted. She decided she would simply have to tolerate any discomfort in the meeting, not somehow avoid it or make it disappear. And in accepting that some awkwardness might present itself, she would persevere regardless.

After stating her needs, her manager said aggressively, "So, you are really going to push this? It just has not been a good time."

Elisa paused. Her manager could see that, this time, she was serious. Then she delivered the response we'd prepared in expectation of that exact statement from her manager: "I don't believe there is ever going to be a good time. So, yes, I need an answer."

It worked. Elisa got the promotion and was promised its completion within six months. Six months later, she was a vice president.

CHAPTER 3

Contained

How Women Are Conditioned to Contain Their Bodies and Voices

How women dress in a professional setting is a tricky topic. There are those who believe that women have lost ground by wearing clothes that some might perceive as too revealing for the workplace, and there are those who believe the mere conversation around telling women how they should dress at work is misogynistic by definition. But from my perspective, to frame the conversation of women's professional dress in terms of sexual liberation or objectification is to miss an entirely different and important point. Yes, your choices about clothing can have serious consequences. But they may not be the ones you think.

The reality is that certain types of clothing restrict women's bodies. This is particularly true if the clothing is tight, short, or low cut, or if heels are too skinny or too high. For example, tight and low-cut shirts mean women have to minimize their gestures. High heels mean women have to take slow and cautious steps. Short skirts mean women have to be wary of them hiking up too high when they sit and cross their legs. These types of restrictions require that women pay more attention to what their movements might reveal and what could trip them up rather than focusing wholly on what they want to say and how they want to say it.

If our bodies are restricted, we can't move freely, take up space, or use large gestures. This also has the effect of restricting our voice in terms of volume, inflection, and emphasis, thereby making it difficult to show conviction and authority or command attention. As long as our bodily movements are restricted, we cannot fully embody presence—that quality we must convey if we want to advance. And, as we will see in this chapter, clothing is but one way culture conditions the containment of our bodies and, in turn, our potential.

A male client of mine appeared on a panel at a tech conference with a female co-panelist and a male moderator. My client and I had devoted recent sessions to preparing him for this event, so I watched the livestream. I took a screenshot of what I observed on the stage because it perfectly captured so much cultural and gender subtext.

The moderator, on the right, is sitting with his legs open. He is leaning forward and resting both elbows on his knees, and his hands are clasped and resting in the space between his legs. He's wearing jeans, a button-down shirt with a cardigan over it, and casual lace-up shoes. He is relaxed and appears at ease.

My client, in the middle, is sitting up comfortably in his chair. His left ankle is crossed over his right knee in a figure-four position. One of his hands rests on his leg. The other hand is on the chair's armrest. He's in a T-shirt, jeans, and sneakers. He also looks relaxed and at ease.

The woman, on the other hand, looks almost like she's at an entirely different conference. She is in a tight purple dress—sleeveless and just-above-the-knee length—with zippers running up the full length of both sides. She's in four-inch heels.

Her legs are pulled tightly together, right down to her feet, to shield the audience's view up her dress. Her arms are pulled into her body, and her hands are held together in a prayer-like position, resting between her knees. She does not look relaxed or at ease. Instead, she looks tucked in and zipped up. She looks physically uncomfortable because the dress so severely restricts her movement, and she must remain conscious of accidentally exposing herself to the audience. Whereas both of the men look confident, her posture looks like that of an obedient schoolgirl.

Gendered Bodies and Voices

During snack time the teacher asks the kids to tell her what they like best in the snack mix. Hillary says, "Marshmallows!" loudly, vigorously, and with a swing of her arm. The teacher turns to her and says, "I'm going to ask you to say that quietly," and Hillary repeats it in a softer voice.[1]

So reads an excerpt about a five-year-old girl from a ground-breaking 1998 paper by Karin A. Martin, professor and chair of the sociology department at the University of Michigan. In "Becoming a Gendered Body: Practices of Preschools," Martin shares the results of observing five preschool classrooms of 112 three- to five-year-olds in a Midwestern city over eight months. Across the classrooms were five head teachers and nine aides, all of whom were female. Of the students, roughly 42 percent were girls, and 58 percent were boys.

By the 1990s, when Martin began her observation of preschool classrooms, many postmodern feminist scholars had been exploring the idea of gender as a function of outward expression (i.e., something we "do"), not a function of our biology (i.e., something that "is"). This idea of gender ran counter to the prevailing notion that the differences in the way women and men use their bodies—to walk, stand, sit, throw, lift, and so on—are innate. The general argument held by these feminist scholars was that bodies used within typical gender expectations further enable and entrench gender hierarchy and stereotypes.

Martin agreed with these scholars. But she noticed that no one was exploring where, how, and when bodies become gendered. Rather, feminists investigating the ways that bodies are gendered and to what effects focused only on adult bodies. If the roots of this gendering went unexplored, Martin argued, then the same scholars looking to debunk the notion of gender as innate risked doing the opposite—confirming the naturalness of typical bodily differences between women and men.[2]

What Martin found in her eight months of observation was unambiguous. Preschool is at least one of the places where bodies are gendered early and often. Specifically, teachers condition little girls to use their bodies in ways that are stereotypically female—quiet, contained, and unimposing; and teachers condition little boys to use their bodies in ways that are stereotypically male—loud, free, big, and imposing.

In "Becoming a Gendered Body," Martin shared selections of the detailed notes she took while watching the teachers and students go about the school day. In one instance, a group of three five-year-old boys was playing with wooden dolls during the class's unstructured playtime. They were engaged in lively imaginative play, pretending that their dolls were jumping off a tower made of wooden blocks and landing on top of each other.

One loudly declared, "I'm the grown-up!" Another chimed in, "I'm the police!" The boys crashed their dolls into each other's and bumped their own bodies into each other. Two more boys joined in, and the already loud play grew louder and the space in which they were playing expanded to fill the center of the classroom. They knocked blocks over, grabbed each other's dolls, hollered with excitement, and began yelling, "Fire! Fire!" In Martin's assessment, the boys were having fun. The teachers allowed their play to go on uninterrupted.

In contrast, three girls, also five years old, were jumping over and around some balls that were rolling between their feet. The girls' mouths were open, and they hummed and giggled with each other as they jumped. Two of the girls stuck out their tongues. Like the boys, the girls were having a great time. That is, until the teacher's aide turned to them and said, "Shhh, find something else to play. Why don't you play Simon Says?"

> Martin's research confirmed that both girls and boys come into the world with the same natural impulse to talk loudly and use their whole bodies to communicate. But our culture reinforces this impulse only for boys.

The girls decided against Simon Says, but they complied with the aide's implied request to play quietly. Crowding around a small desk, the girls began sorting Legos, soft blocks, and puzzle pieces to "help" the aide. As they tidied up, they giggled with each other, covering their mouths with their hands to muffle the sound, and whispered into each other's ears. Martin notes that by limiting the girls' voices, the teacher's aide also limited the use of their bodies, as they were now using only their hands to play instead of their legs, feet, and whole bodies.

These limiting directives toward girls were the norm of Martin's observations. Teachers consistently quieted girls' voices and bodies. They consistently gave boys much more leeway to use their voices loudly and use their whole bodies to play and express themselves. Martin's research confirmed that both girls and boys come into the world with the same natural impulse to talk loudly and use their whole bodies to communicate. But our culture reinforces this impulse only for boys.

How Women Are Conditioned to Be Contained

Martin's research explains some of the origins of containment of women's bodies and voices in our adult lives, which I see day in and day out in my work with female clients. Her research, along with others' research that has arrived at similar conclusions, shows us that girls' bodies and voices are gendered and conditioned in five distinct ways:

1)   Girls are conditioned to contain their bodies so that they are small and take up less space.

At the 2010 TEDWomen conference, Sheryl Sandberg, COO of Facebook, spoke about the dearth of female leaders and why this must change. This appearance at TEDWomen was viewed by millions, helping to solidify her status as a rising star. (Her first book, *Lean In*, would be published in 2013.)

When I loaded her TED Talk on my laptop to watch it for the first time, I was excited to see what she had to say. Except I found myself distracted and unable to focus on her message. Sandberg wore a tight top that made movement from her shoulders difficult. She was in a fitted skirt that shortened her steps. She teetered in four-inch heels that caused her occasional movement across the stage to be tentative, as not to lose her balance or trip. Her dress was relatively conservative—while it was form-fitting, she was showing little skin. But it was blatantly restrictive and therefore contained her movements, ease, and comfort on stage and the overall impact of her presence. Instead of listening to her message, I was fixated on the irony of a woman talking about women's empowerment while stitched into a restrictive casing that disempowered her body and voice's full expression.

Restrictive, uncomfortable, burdensome, hot, and physically constraining dress is nothing new for women. We used to put women in dangerous corsets that would displace ribs, drop blood pressure, squash lungs, compress other organs, impair breathing, and hinder digestion, among other torturous effects—simply to make them look impossibly small. It can be easy to observe women walking around in whatever they please and think our work liberating women's dress is done. When we go to our closets, we likely see everything from dresses and skirts to pants and shorts to blouses and T-shirts to sandals, heels, flats, and sneakers—and we are free to select from any and all of them.

Yet many women fail to consider how certain kinds of dress restrict our bodies and the overall effect this has on how we move. And why wouldn't we fail to notice this? Restrictive attire has been women's reality since our youngest years. It may be all we know.

How children are clothed for preschool is, of course, informed by societal norms of dress for girls and boys and usually decided by parents. The clothes they wear to school impact the experiences they have in class and at play. Repeatedly, Martin saw girls in dresses that limited their physicality. She believes it's not the dress itself that restrains bodies, but an already developed awareness of how one is supposed to move and behave in a dress. In one instance, Martin watched a five-year-old girl in a dress bend over to look at something, which exposed some of her back. A female classmate then pulled down the girl's dress and gave it a pat to keep it in place, as a mother might do. Girls often wear tights under their dresses, which require constant rearranging, pulling, and fixing. On multiple occasions, Martin watched girls fidget with their clothing in an attempt to make them feel more comfortable on their bodies. She did not observe boys doing the same. Martin repeatedly watched as particular items of clothing made "girls' movements smaller, leading girls to take up less space with their bodies and disallowing some types of movements."[3] As I like to say, you can't climb a tree in a dress, and you can't run in sparkly imitations of the ruby slippers Dorothy wore in *The Wizard of Oz*.

2) *Girls are conditioned to contain the use of their bodies to fit the preferences and instructions of others.*

Girls' fashion-oriented clothing (think big ruffled dresses, bows, large hair clips) had another alarming effect, in that it appears to permit a sense of agency over girls' bodies. Martin noted an incident where one of the five-year-old boys lifted a girl's dress to her embarrassment. The teacher told the boy to stop, "and that was the end of it." Yet Martin observed teachers doing the same thing to girls in dresses; she watched as they lifted their skirts to see if their diapers were wet, to see if they had warm clothes on underneath, to see if their clothes needed rearranging, and so on. In almost all cases, teachers did this without first asking the girl's permission and in front of other students. Martin refers to this as "management" of the girl rather than an interaction with her. Teachers were much more inclined to "manage" girls—tuck in their shirts, fix a bow in their hair, tighten their ponytails, rearrange their clothing—than they were boys. What girls learn when teachers (and others in society) touch their clothes and adornments is that their bodies are, at least to a degree, under the management of others. Others have some permission to touch or blatantly observe our bodies. Women, then, become conditioned to expect that there is an ever-watchful eye on our bodies, which serves to keep our own attention disproportionately on our appearances and how they may be perceived by others.

Perhaps not surprising in a classroom full of wiggly preschoolers, teachers are constantly giving students instructions for their bodies. Of the many bodily orders Martin logged, 65 percent were given to boys, 26 percent to girls, and 9 percent to mixed groups. While teachers did much more disciplining of boys' bodies than of girls', how they did it is what's relevant. Typically, teachers told boys to stop using their bodies in some way, like running or pushing. But the order would end there. This was not the case with the girls. Almost always, teachers told girls *how* to move their bodies instead. For example, if a teacher asked a boy to stop throwing a ball, the order would end there. If a teacher asked a girl to stop throwing a ball, she would also ask the girl to pick it up and put it away. Teachers proved much more comfortable giving girls additional directives and instructions. Furthermore, if teachers' requests to boys to stop a bodily behavior went ignored, most of the time they never took further action. By contrast, girls almost always obeyed the teacher's direction the first time.

Martin's conclusion is that boys are left with a large set of options for how they might use their bodies. In other words, boys maintained a greater sense of ownership over their bodily movements and bodies in general. Girls, by contrast, were more compliant with their teachers' directions and more willing to confine their bodies to satisfy teacher requests. With this kind of repeated socialization, we have to imagine that little girls steadily lose a sense of agency over their own bodies. We have to imagine that, long before they can grasp the implications, they learn that instructions from others for how to use their bodies—including by the forceful touch of others' hands on them—are to be expected, accepted, and followed.

> **Martin found that teachers told girls to be quiet or repeat something in a quieter, "nicer" voice three times the rate they told boys.**

3) *Girls are conditioned to contain and quiet their voices, which naturally contains and quiets their bodies.*

Remember Hillary from earlier in the chapter, the five-year-old who "loudly, vigorously, and with a swing of her arm" declared her love of marshmallows? When she restated her love of marshmallows, per her teacher's request, Martin notes that she did so in a quiet voice and with no bodily movement. Martin saw a clear link between quiet voices and "quiet" bodies.

Overwhelmingly, teachers disciplined girls' voices, but they did not discipline boys' voices. Martin found that teachers told girls to be quiet or repeat something in a quieter, "nicer" voice three times the rate they told boys—despite the fact that boys' play was typically far louder than the girls' play. To emphasize this data when giving talks or guiding workshops, I often show the corresponding table from Martin's paper because it is so staggering. Of all commands to be quiet that the teachers gave, the recipients were girls a stunning 73 percent of the time.

Observations of Teachers Telling Children to Be Quiet, by Gender of Child: Five Preschool Classrooms

Gender	N	Percent
Girls	45	73
Boys	16	26
Total	61	100

Source: "Becoming a Gendered Body: Practices of Preschools," Karin A. Martin

In the rare instances that boys were asked to quiet down, they were usually in groups. Martin rarely saw a teacher tell an individual boy to say something nicely and quietly. Where boys were allowed to use their whole bodies and a range of vocal volume to convey all manner of emotions, girls were left with only the stifled flatness of a nice, quiet voice. When girls become women who communicate with these learned quiet voices and reserved bodies, they appear less convicted and without authority or command. They have internalized the containment of their bodies and are left with few communication tools to fully express the extent of their ideas, decisions, requests, and directions.

4) *Girls are conditioned to contain their so-called "negative" emotions.*

> *Keith is persistently threatening to knock over the building that Amy built. He is running around her with a "flying" toy horse that comes dangerously close to her building each time. She finally says, "Stop it!" in a loud voice. The teacher comes over and asks, "How do we say that, Amy?" Amy looks at Keith and says more softly, "Stop trying to knock it over." The teacher tells Keith to find someplace else to play.* (Five-year-olds)

Martin observed an additional and disturbing consequence of the expectation that girls speak quietly and nicely: Girls were steadily trained out of one of their primary mechanisms for "resisting others' mistreatment of them." That is, they were conditioned to suppress their anger, frustration, or sense of violation. And then they were conditioned not to use a loud, stern, commanding voice or their body language to show their frustration, anger, or sense of violation in an attempt to protect or defend themselves. When a girl had a disagreement with a classmate, Martin watched teachers ask the girl to "quiet down" and "solve the problem nicely." Teachers would only intervene in boys' disagreements if they escalated. While teachers did instruct boys to talk things out, Martin never saw teachers instruct them to do so quietly. As a byproduct, boys' anger and frustration are enabled and encouraged. This fact has its downsides as well, as it is a missed opportunity for boys to learn to regulate their anger.

For girls, the effect of shaming and silencing their anger is the dismantling of not only their natural reflex to self-protect but also the sense that they are entitled to do so. In *Rage Becomes Her*, author and feminist activist Soraya Chemaly writes, "By effectively severing anger from 'good womanhood,' we choose to sever girls and women from the emotion that best protects us against danger and injustice."[4] Instead, the conditioned containment of a girl's voice and body is expected to remain intact even if she is mistreated, disrespected, or violated. The girls' emphasis, once again, is put on how the other feels, even if the "other" is an offender or perpetrator.

Chemaly notes another sinister side effect of robbing girls of the emphatic use of their voices and bodies to show anger and defend themselves: Girls begin to perceive disruptive behaviors and assertiveness as "linguistic markers of masculinity."[5] In learning to contain our so-called "negative" emotions—such as anger, indignation, and frustration—we are also learning that to be angry is to be masculine. As we saw in Chapter 2, women will—subconsciously or otherwise—defer, demean, and deny themselves in order to avoid punishment for not being perceived as feminine. Suppression of our anger is another way we might protect a perception of femininity, even if we simultaneously fail to protect our whole selves and bodies.

Yet all humans obviously feel anger. So what do women do with theirs? In one study cited by Chemaly in *Rage Becomes*

Her, researchers found that while men are allowed and even encouraged to express anger, women are not—but they are allowed to express sadness. As a result, women learn early on to transmute their anger into sadness in order to remain socially acceptable and avoid a negative response from others. The problem with this, Chemaly notes, is twofold. First, women lose the opportunity to productively express and utilize their anger, and the results can be debilitating or even catastrophic; festering anger has been linked to physical health issues, depression, and anxiety. Second, sadness is perceived as weak and submissive. Whereas anger is associated with control and power, which are critical components of leadership, sadness is associated with powerlessness and pessimism.[6] Anger is an emotion that precedes and is necessary for action, while sadness is often coupled with acceptance and passivity. Severing girls early from their anger safeguards the status quo.[7] If women are sad, they are likely not trying to rock the patriarchal boat. And they are likely not fighting for the promotion they deserve or for pay commensurate with that of their male counterparts. In effect, if women are sad, they run the risk of continued mistreatment.

5) *Girls are conditioned to contain the space and time they take up and cede it to others, namely boys.*

At the beginning of the chapter, I mentioned the group of boys whom Martin observed playing raucously with their wooden dolls in the center of the classroom. As they played without interruption, the teacher's aide told a group of girls giggling and jumping around rolling balls to play something quieter. The girls then hovered around the space of a desk as they helped the teacher tidy up toys. Whereas the girls were relegated to one little area just larger than the size of a desk, the boys continued to play at full volume with their blocks in the entire center of the room. Martin concluded that schools were not only gendering bodies, but they were also gendering space: Boys are permitted and even encouraged to take up more of it, and girls are often instructed to take up less.

In 2003, Lia Karsten, a professor of behavioral sciences at the University of Amsterdam, sought to further investigate how girls and boys relate to the space around them and how entitled they feel to use it. She observed children on eight different public playgrounds—spaces that, she rightly assumed, could reveal much about how girls and boys orient themselves spatially relative to each other. She found that the girls tended to cluster in smaller groups on the periphery of the playgrounds, whereas boys would run all over the entire expanse of them.[8] In a separate study of girls' and boys' play spaces, gender studies professor Barrie Thorne found that it was typical for boys to interrupt girls in their playtime and invade the small spaces they were using, but the converse was not common.[9]

Such patterns of boys encroaching on girls' space and the expectation that girls will defer their space to them are seen throughout childhood. Martin explores this phenomenon through "formal and relaxed behaviors." In preschool, formal behaviors include expectations such as raising one's hand before speaking, sitting on one's bottom, and sitting upright in a chair. We can think of these as polite, unimposing behaviors that contain how a girl uses the space around her and her voice.

Relaxed behaviors include crawling, lying down when the instructor is teaching, and running indoors—all behaviors that take up space. In the earliest years of preschool, boys were encouraged to engage in relaxed behaviors more often. Girls were encouraged to be formal most of the time. Through different behavioral standards for girls and boys, Martin believes teachers help construct and reinforce the expectation that "boys will be boys." That is, teachers help enable the perception that boys are less controllable and the belief that there's less use in trying to control them.

Myra Sadker and David Sadker, both advocates for education equality, were curious to see if and how teachers continue to treat girls and boys differently throughout all school. Sadker and Sadker spent two decades researching gender bias in schools and its toxic effects on schools' capacity to deliver girls the same education they deliver to boys. They compiled their robust research in *Failing at Fairness: How Our Schools Cheat Girls*, in which they wrote:

> *Sometimes what they [boys] say has little or nothing to do with the teacher's questions. Whether male comments are insightful or irrelevant, teachers respond to them. However, when girls call out, there is a fascinating occurrence: Suddenly the teacher remembers the rule about raising your hand before you talk.*[10]

Generally, there is a compelling body of evidence that shows girls have not been treated equally in public schools and have not received the same quality, or even quantity, of education as their male peers. One such study, "How Schools Shortchange Girls," commissioned by the American Association of University Women Educational Foundation and researched by the Wellesley College Center for Research on Women, discovered that girls and boys entered public schools essentially equal in measured ability. Twelve years later, girls left school having fallen behind their male classmates and with two times the self-confidence loss of boys.[11] This is true even though girls have for decades earned better grades than boys in all subjects and, on paper, often appear "ahead" of boys upon graduation. That girls have, in fact, fallen behind on several metrics is in part attributable to teachers' gender bias, in which teachers: 1) systematically discourage girls from taking courses essential to their future employability and economic well-being; 2) spend

> By restricting the duration of girls' talking time, teachers subtly condition students that girls' voices and ideas matter less than boys' voices and ideas and should therefore be "contained."

significantly more time with boys than with girls; 3) permit boys in elementary and middle school to call out answers eight times more often than girls, while discouraging girls from calling out answers without first raising their hands; 4) encourage boys to speak more often than they encourage girls to speak; and 5) are more likely to interrupt girls than they are boys.[12]

Girls in school are literally given less time and fewer opportunities to speak, whereas boys are given the floor more often and are able to talk longer by virtue of being interrupted less. By restricting the duration of girls' talking time, teachers subtly condition students that girls' voices and ideas matter less than boys' voices and ideas and should therefore be "contained."[13] It should be no surprise to learn that girls who graduate from all-girls high schools report more confidence overall and rate their public speaking and writing skills more favorably than do their counterparts at coed schools.[14]

When girls internalize their biased treatment in school for twelve, sixteen, or even twenty years, they begin to believe that the public domain belongs to men, not to women. They also feel that the public domain is not safe for women. A lack of practice engaging in the public domain leaves girls more susceptible to the belief that their ideas hold less value and are less worthy of being shared than boys' ideas. When we assert our ideas or engage with confidence, we are made to feel like we are imposing on a sphere that is not ours to own. So, too often, we simply do not assert our ideas.

Containment Inhibits Our Adult Bodies and Limits Our Careers

The most effective leaders have an abundant supply of "executive presence"—that elusive quality that is in high demand at senior levels of organizations. What does it mean to have presence? Sylvia Ann Hewlett—an economist, expert on gender and workplace issues, and founding president of the Center for Talent Innovation—sought to bring tangibility to this intangible quality. She and her team surveyed 4,000 college-educated professionals, including 268 senior executives, on what it means to embody executive presence. While the finer details of executive presence vary by industry and context, Hewlett found that it invariably has three pillars: 1) gravitas, or how you act; 2) communication, or how you speak; and 3) appearance, or how you look.

The three pillars are the focal point of Hewlett's 2014 book, *Executive Presence: The Missing Link Between Merit and Success*. Not all three pillars are created equal; of the 268 senior executives surveyed, 67 percent voted gravitas as the most important pillar, 28 percent voted communication as the most important, and only 5 percent voted appearance as the most important pillar.[15]

Let's dig deeper on what gravitas means, according to Hewlett's research. Gravitas is one's capacity to command a room and convey the authority of a leader. Hewlett found that "intellectual horsepower," knowing "your stuff cold," and being able to speak "six questions deep" in one's knowledge domain underpin gravitas—but they do not define it. Gravitas is projecting confidence and credibility when communicating knowledge and winning buy-in, especially in challenging times. Among the components of gravitas, the senior executives named "grace under fire" as the most important for embodying executive presence.[16] When we think about grace under fire, we think of those who fully inhabit their bodies and themselves with an ease, a comfort, a certitude, and—when necessary—courage. We think of an unflappable poise and self-assurance.

> **Effective leaders have an abundant supply of "executive presence"—that elusive quality that is in high demand at senior levels of organizations.**

The senior executive survey respondents reported that speaking skills are central to the communication pillar of executive presence. This includes how one uses voice, posture, and body language in order to captivate an audience—of one or thousands.[16] Eye contact was found to be pivotal to creating buy-in and inspiring an audience when giving presentations or selling ideas.

By contrast, those with low presence tend to do the opposite.

They speak quietly. They tuck in their bodies, make them small, and try to take up as little space as possible. They struggle with eye contact when talking to others. And when they speak, it is with a measured assertiveness, if there is any assertiveness at all.

Presence matters. A lot. In Hewlett's research, the senior leaders she surveyed said that presence accounts for at least 26 percent of what it takes to be worthy of advancement to senior levels.[17] In a different survey out of the Stanford VMware Women's Leadership Innovation Lab, 240 senior leaders in Silicon Valley rated visibility as the most important criterion of promotion to senior levels.[18] The two go hand-in-hand—those with presence have the wherewithal to make themselves visible; and the more visible one is, the more opportunities they have to practice, embody, and convey presence. When I ask the managers of my female clients what in their view is holding back my client most from a promotion, overwhelmingly I hear, "She lacks presence and visibility."

Let's revisit the photo of my client and two other people onstage at the conference. The men are unapologetically taking up space. Just like the preschool boys in Martin's observations, they are relaxed. The woman looks formal, stiff, and uncomfortable. She has made herself as small as possible. In doing so, she is demonstrating low-status bodily behavior that projects insecurity, when in fact the exact opposite is true. She is, after all, a CEO of a successful venture firm. When she spoke, her confidence was evident. However, her body language was telling a different story.

As women learn, if even bit by bit, to assert themselves such that they win promotions, they typically experience small boosts in confidence. This can make the next instance where they must assert themselves feel a little less daunting or improbable, which can then unlock another small confidence boost. Typically, what I see as women advance in their careers is that they gain piecemeal boosts in confidence. Rarely does a woman instantly shed all her decades of conditioning with just one successful negotiation or confrontational conversation. Rarely does a woman, in one fell swoop, go from hesitant to having gravitas. It is therefore not atypical to see female senior leaders still comport their bodies in insecure ways or feel tentative using their voices loudly and with conviction.

Of all the ways women are conditioned and constrained, the discomfort using their bodies to communicate can be the most difficult to overcome. Instead of trying to push through the discomfort to practice and achieve high-status body language skills, many women resign themselves to their discomfort, saying they're just not gifted speakers. Or they don't like public speaking, so what does it matter. Or they'd rather not be the one to give the presentation anyway because they are uncomfortable being the center of attention. What they fail to see is that not fully and comfortably inhabiting one's body can itself cause one to feel less confident.[19] Our contained bodies put a ceiling on our confidence *and* our potential. It is a catch-22, and the only way out is to tolerate the discomfort of using one's body until it becomes less uncomfortable and more familiar.

> Our contained bodies put a ceiling on our confidence *and* our potential.

Contained bodies and voices show up in our professional lives in a multitude of ways. This is what I have seen in my twenty-plus years of observing women in professional settings.

Women will:

- Voluntarily sit in the outside row of seats against the wall, not at the table, in meetings.
- Stay seated when presenting. If a woman co-presents with a man, she tends to defer more of the time to her partner. She will also stand slightly behind him, even when she is speaking.
- Stand toward the back, not the front, of the stage or room.
- Speak quietly to avoid imposing her "loud" voice on others.
- Speak for less time compared to men to avoid feeling like they are imposing on others' time. They will even sacrifice stating all of their ideas or explaining them fully to speak for less time.
- Not state their ideas in meetings or to large groups, choosing instead to share them with an individual or a smaller group later.
- Speak less and listen more in meetings than men do. This can risk no longer being invited to meetings.
- Back down from making their points, especially if they are interrupted. Women tend not to push back or correct the record, leaving their points and ideas to remain unfinished or misinterpreted in others' minds.
- Wear restrictive clothing that constrains their physicality, making it difficult to exude confidence and convey presence. When women present or speak, restrictive clothing can make them appear stiff and more formal and stifled

in their movement. (FYI: While over 75 percent of those 268 senior executives surveyed about executive presence said that unkempt attire undercuts women's and men's executive presence, 73 percent of them also said too-tight or provocative clothing detracts from it.[20])

- Be less demonstrative, and therefore less engaging, when they speak. Women do not use their voices' full range of volume and inflection, nor do they use many hand movements or facial expressions to animate their speech. (FYI: Research has found that an average of 14 gestures per minute increases one's persuasiveness, but only when gestures are "illustrative," "ideational," and correlated to language.[21]) Women are less likely to own or occupy the space around them.
- Make less eye contact and hold it for shorter amounts of time.
- Suppress and not communicate their anger in the workplace. This can have the unintended consequence of enabling situations that make women angry or leave them treated unfairly.

Each of these behaviors falls in line with how we were conditioned to comport our bodies and use our voices. But they fall far outside the line of leadership and the demonstrations of presence, authority, credibility, and the ability to influence others that must precede promotions to senior levels. As a culmination of our contained bodies, we are more likely to be told we lack the presence and the visibility necessary to advance.

Un-Containing and Reclaiming Our Bodies and Voices

To free ourselves from containment, we must free up our bodies and voices.

In 1980, Iris Marion Young, who served as a professor of political science at the University of Chicago, wrote a seminal essay unpacking the phenomenon of gendered bodies. "Throwing Like a Girl: A Phenomenology of Feminine Body Comportment Motility and Spatiality" offers a meticulous analysis of the differences in women's and men's gross motor movements to complete a task, such as throwing a baseball or lifting something heavy. Young says of women's movement: "Not only is there a typical style of throwing like a girl, but there is a more or less typical style of running like a girl, climbing like a girl, swinging like a girl, hitting like a girl."[22] This "typical style," she notes, is tentative, almost fearful. Unlike men, Young says, the women rarely used the full force and potential of their bodies to complete physical tasks. As an example, if a woman lifted something heavy, she most likely used only the extremities directly involved in the task—her hands and arms as opposed to summoning the additional strength of her back, core, and legs. Young writes:

> Women often approach a physical engagement with things with timidity, uncertainty, and hesitancy. Typically, we lack an entire trust in our bodies to carry us to our aims. There is, I suggest, a double hesitation here. On the one hand, we often lack confidence that we have the capacity to do what must be done...The other side of this tentativeness is, I suggest, a fear of getting hurt, which is greater in women than in men...We often experience our bodies as a fragile encumbrance, rather than the

media for the enactment of our aims.[23]

She goes on to say, "All the above factors operate to produce in many women a greater or lesser feeling of incapacity, frustration, and self-consciousness." In being told again and again as girls to "sit quietly," "be still," "walk don't run," "don't get dirty," "don't play rough," "don't throw that," "be nice," "act like a lady," and "dress nicely," we have been systematically disenfranchised from our own bodies. We have been robbed of opportunities to experiment with them, discover their strength, understand that they are not fragile, and learn that they can get hurt and recover. Without remediation, our use of our bodies is detached from reality—the reality that they have the same potential as men's to be strong, capable, and resilient. Detachment from this reality of our bodies detaches us *from* our bodies.

> In being told again and again as girls to "sit quietly," "be still," "walk don't run," "don't get dirty," "don't play rough," "don't throw that," "be nice," "act like a lady," and "dress nicely," we have been systematically disenfranchised from our own bodies.

It's important to note that, since Young's 1980 essay, much has changed about the perceptions of women's bodies and strength. The idea of a fragile, delicate woman trying and failing to lift a moving box surely seems preposterous to most of us. It is also much more likely we understand today that it's not the box that could injure us, it's failing to recruit the full strength of our bodies to lift the box. But there was no Serena Williams or Mia Hamm in 1980 serving as a model of what women's bodies can do. Today, young girls are actively encouraged to be athletic and play sports. We ourselves might be athletic, lift weights, run marathons, cycle for miles, swim long distances, and feel strong.

But I believe we have to consider if our comfort using our bodies at the gym comes with us into the conference room. When we change out of our flexible gym clothes and into a tight skirt and high heels, we lose our flexibility to move, gesture, and express ourselves fully.

By now you should be well convinced that how you may or may not use your body in your professional life is a function of conditioning. Young believed—as I hope you do, too—this detachment from our bodies is only psychological. There is no genetic or constitutional basis behind it. To own our bodies and also liberate our voices, we have to change our mindsets about them first.

Changing Our Minds to Change Our Bodies and Voices to Change Our Minds

Martin's research shows us how natural the full use of our bodies and voices to express ourselves authentically actually is. It is all the ways society denies women the use of their bodies and voices that is unnatural. Once we have this insight, we can and will develop presence. We can reclaim our bodies and voices and discover how our comfort with them can impact the advancement of our careers.

Almost every time I begin guiding a female client to un-contain her body, she is uncomfortable. First, I remind her that some fear and anxiety is totally normal, as the detachment from our bodies is deep-seated. Any movement that begins to break the seal of our containment will of course feel foreign and maybe even frightening. Second, I remind her that we can do things to scale back our fear and anxiety about fully inhabiting our bodies and the space around us. We can practice, until it begins to feel a bit more natural, and a bit more natural, and a bit more natural, until we feel—*it is natural*!

Then I will usually ask the client to do some power poses—an idea that went mainstream with Amy Cuddy's 2012 TED Talk, "Your Body Language May Shape Who You Are." A social psychologist, Cuddy had conducted research that found that when people take expansive postures, it can raise testosterone and lower cortisol. As it turns out, this is the hormonal state of the most effective and empowered leaders. Pointing to research that women tend to make themselves small, Cuddy specifically calls on them—as well as all disempowered or under-resourced people—to use power poses to reclaim their inherent power.

Once the idea of power posing had gone mainstream—thanks to the popularity of Cuddy's TED Talk, which, as of this writing, remains the second-most-watched TED Talk of all time—several people challenged her hormone research. They argued that her research methodologies were not replicable and her conclusions therefore dubious. While constructive criticism is part of the scientific process, the feedback went far beyond the merits of her scientific conclusions, with multiple people levying personal attacks on Cuddy herself. In the end, the impact of power posing on one's hormonal state has yet to be replicated. However, multiple replicable studies before and since Cuddy's TED Talk have found that power posing boosts one's sense of power, confidence, and success potential. The subjective experience of feeling "more confident" due to power posing has been replicated and remains valid.[24]

Anecdotally, I have lived and witnessed how power posing has the potential to liberate women's bodies and voices. I have seen this liberation help women feel more powerful, act more powerfully, and speak with more power. Hormone levels aside, power posing works.

As clients grow more comfortable inhabiting and fully utilizing their bodies and voices, they so often tell me how exciting and empowering it is. This is because they have broken psychological and cultural constraints that have kept their bodies and voices small, quiet, and unimposing their entire lives. I can see it change their confidence and increase their presence—that unapologetic capacity to take up space and communicate with their whole bodies and voices. There is nothing more satisfying than seeing a once-tentative woman thoroughly enjoy taking to the front of the room and taking full command of it.

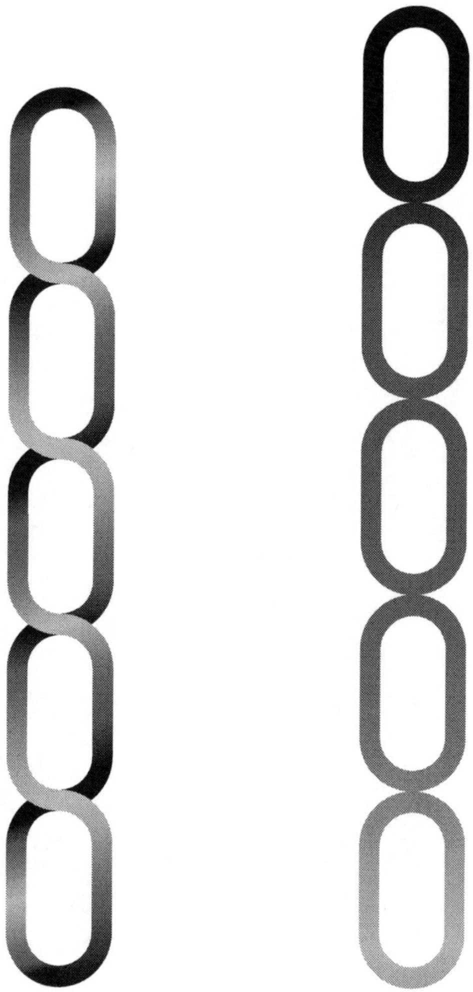

CHAPTER 4

Collaborative

How Women Are Conditioned to Prioritize Collaboration Over Hierarchy

I love to swim. When I was ten, I started swimming competitively. Since then, if there is a pool in the vicinity, I will be there. Soon after I had my second child, I decided to join a U.S. Masters Swim team with 22 women and two men. With our coach, we've been training at the same swim club, three times a week, for fifteen years. Everyone at the club knows that on Monday, Wednesday, and Friday, the pool is reserved for the Masters team from 6:30 a.m. to 7:30 a.m.

Typically, the swimmers before us wrap up their swim a couple of minutes prior to our start time. Many years ago, one swimmer—a man—would never get out of the pool by 6:30 a.m. When he would get close to the wall during his designated swim time, he would lift his head out of the water as he turned around, rather than doing a "flip" turn, in which your head remains underwater. But, miraculously, at 6:25 a.m., minutes before our team's turn, his skills would improve. He would remain underwater for his turns, making it difficult to get his attention as our time approached. On many days, he kept up this routine well past 6:30 a.m.

One morning, irritated with this man's infringement on our time, I jumped into the lane next to his and waited until he was at the wall. I leaned over the lane rope, got very close to him, and raised my voice: "I hate to say it, but I think it's our time to get in the pool."

He lifted his head as he made his turn and said, "Got it." Yet he proceeded to keep swimming! Now I was mad.

A teammate of mine walked toward his lane. I watched to see how she would handle him. When he approached the wall, she leaned down close to his head and yelled, "You're about to jump out, right?"

No surprise, he ignored her and kept on swimming!

In jumped another teammate, who swam over to the lane line closest to him, as I had, but stopped short of swimming into his lane. At this point, I was fascinated by the whole situation—what would she say? How would he react to a third woman approaching him? As he completed his turn, she shook the lane line and then yelled, "Do you know what time it is?" He raised his hand as if to signal he'd heard her, but the man kept on swimming. It was now 6:33 a.m.

Our coach, Judy, was standing across the pool, where she'd been taking in the entire scene. As the man swam toward her end of the pool, she pulled a bright yellow kickboard from the bin, walked over to the end of his lane, and just before he turned, stuck the board down in the water smack in front of his face. It startled him. He planted his feet on the bottom of the pool and looked up at her with feigned bewilderment.

"It's our time," Judy said bluntly. "We're getting in."

She then signaled me to get into his lane and called for the first round of swimmers on our team to hop into theirs. She meant business, and backed up her decisive action with clear, decisive language.

It worked. He got out.

When we are conditioned to consider others' feelings and experiences before our own, and when we are conditioned to contain our voices and bodies, the way we speak is deformed, contorted, and obscured. My swim story perfectly illustrates the effect of women's conditioning on our conversational style. My teammates and I had the same goal as Judy, but we used ineffective language to express it.

By the end of this chapter, you'll understand the ways my two teammates and I "bubble wrapped" or neutralized our speech in order to make it apologetic, unimposing, and polite. I suspect that you will start to see all the ways you bubble wrap your speech to blunt sharp edges and tones, particularly when under stress or feeling vulnerable. You will also see that women have learned to modify their speech in order to protect themselves from a culture that can punish them for deviating from the confines of femininity. In some cases, this adaptation is brilliant—a true superpower that, when used strategically and intentionally, can help us get what we want without making others feel threatened and motivated to retaliate. But, in our careers, this superpower can become a liability in situations that require assertiveness and directness. Too often, we tone down our communication out of unconscious habit, leaving us to appear weak or powerless when we need to look decisive and authoritative.

> Too often, we tone down our communication out of unconscious habit, leaving us to appear weak or powerless when we need to look decisive and authoritative.

When Considerate and Contained Meet Conversational Style

The difference in how women and men ask for directions is so universally understood that the mere mention of it can get a knowing laugh from any audience. The typical story goes that men insist they are not lost and resist asking for directions for as long as possible. If they must admit defeat and seek help, men couch their question in terms like "I know where I am, but the house numbers around here are unreadable." Women, on the other hand, will ask for directions as soon as they realize they are lost. Upon finding someone who can help, a woman might preface her question with something like "I'm so sorry to bother you. I'm lost, could you help me?"

Deborah Tannen, a professor and prolific author, has devoted her career to studying how gender affects conversational styles from childhood to adulthood. As a linguist, she analyzes language within a larger social, cultural, and historical context. These contextual forces determine the underlying linguistic patterns that shape how one speaks, whether a person is aware of it or not. Tannen observed key differences in how women and men approach and engage in conversation. For example, she attributes the male way of asking for directions to men's sensitivity to social power dynamics. Her research shows that men operate in a world of hierarchy and have a preoccupation with protecting and promoting their status.[1] To admit to being lost is to acknowledge lower status relative to the person being asked for help. Women operate in a world of collaboration, which leads them to be preoccupied with protecting and promoting peace and harmony. To interrupt someone's day to ask for directions might be to impose upon or offend that person.

While men and women share the same goal when asking for directions, their approaches serve different needs.

Tannen traces the linguistic patterns of men and women to how we learn to converse with friends as children. Children tend to play in same-sex groups, which creates and reinforces gendered speaking patterns that carry into adulthood.

Tannen observed that boys tend to play in large groups.[2] While more boys are included, they are by no means equal. The emphasis in boys' groups is on hierarchy and chain of command. There is at least one leader, and the expectation is for them to demonstrate leadership by giving orders and directions, particularly to those with lower status in the group. Boys jockey for status by showcasing skills and knowledge, telling jokes or stories, or giving or resisting challenges. They use a particular conversational style that signals and negotiates their status. They also learn how to talk "up" and "down" to those with more and less status, respectively.

Girls' playgroups look very different. According to Tannen, girls tend to play with one close friend or in small groups. Talking features prominently in girls' play, and it is often used to create and affirm a sense of inclusion, intimacy, and collaboration. In groups, girls work hard to downplay any appearance of hierarchy and instead focus on what makes them similar, not different. Any woman who attended middle school can attest that girls will often ostracize other girls who appear too confident or believe they are superior in any way. Same goes for girls who issue too many directives. Egalitarianism becomes a central objective of girls' dialogue.

The adult world mirrors how girls and boys play and

communicate as kids. Language researcher and professor Carole Edelsky saw similarly gendered patterns among her female and male university colleagues in their academic committee meetings. In her 1981 paper, "Who's Got the Floor?" she reported that two kinds of speaking typically happened in the meetings. The first was somewhat more formal, where one person would "hold the floor" and speak essentially in monologue, often for long amounts of time. Another person would speak only when it was clear that the prior speaker was finished. She labeled this the "singly developed floor" and shorthanded it "F1." The second kind of speaking was more casual, where people would speak for short amounts of time and chime in when they had something to add in a sort of free-for-all. Edelsky labeled this a "collaborative floor" and shorthanded it "F2." Men dominated F1 talking time and were much more comfortable speaking at length than the women were—if women spoke at all. In F2, women and men spoke in more equal measure.[3]

When considering the underlying dynamics of F1 and F2, the different behaviors of women and men make sense. F1 is hierarchical and competitive, where the floor is won or lost and attention is squarely on the person who has the floor. F1 is a circumstance in which women are less comfortable and have learned it can be problematic or unsafe to participate. By contrast, F2 offers circumstances that are safer and far more appealing for women. In Edelsky's words, F2 conversations are "cooperative ventures that provide both a cover of 'anonymity' for assertive language use and a comfortable backdrop against which women can display a fuller range of language ability."[4] In other words, when multiple people contribute to a faster-paced conversation, women feel more comfortable using an assertive conversational style because their statements will be less scrutinized.

Edelsky's work sheds light on something crucial to acknowledge about women's linguistic patterns: They are adaptive and designed to protect us. They are a predictable outcome of how we are conditioned.

The Considerate constraint encourages girls to sacrifice their personal agency in order to consider others first. Living with only partial agency is a vulnerable place for women to be. Girls learn to define themselves in terms of how they relate to others and how others perceive them relative to feminine expectations. We learn to prioritize being likable over and above our ambitions, our ideas, and our dreams. Instead of embodying all that we are, we defer, demean, and deny parts of ourselves so that we fit the confines of what is expected of us as girls and eventually women.

The Contained constraint distorts our relationship with our bodies and voices, thus interfering with how we communicate and interact with others. We learn to make our bodies small and unimposing so as not to offend or inconvenience anyone with our presence. When we do this, our voices follow suit, growing quiet, unassuming, and polite in tone. We internalize and follow the directives of others as to how we can and cannot use our bodies. This often includes subtle or explicit messages to cede to others the space our bodies could otherwise occupy and the length of time we could otherwise use to speak. We begin to grasp that to be angry is to be masculine and that our anger might upset others or make them uncomfortable. So we learn to transform it into something less threatening, less imposing—

usually sadness, which subdues our bodies, voices, and anger reflex.

With constraints that converge to curtail our sense of agency and ownership over our bodies and voices, it is easier and safer to focus on egalitarianism, peace, and inclusion. So we learn to use a conversational style to advance these goals. If we are taught to believe we cannot defend ourselves from threats or reprisal when we behave in ways contrary to our conditioning, we'd be wise to use all of our skills and communication tools to gather allies who can help.

Feminine conditioning has taught us to leverage empathy and an inclusive conversational style, often for our own safety and in many cases to our benefit. Yet for those of us looking to advance in our careers, the downsides of our conditioning cannot be ignored. The constraints on our sense of self, our bodies, and how we speak have held us back. To the extent that our conditioned speaking patterns remain unconscious, our options are limited and our conversational style one-dimensional. If the only speech we have is collaborative, then how can we speak authoritatively and decisively? How can we show leadership when we have only a communication style that is watered down, lacking assertiveness, or deferential when it needs to be authoritative? How can we embody presence and command attention when we have only "I hate to say it, but I think it is our time to get in the pool" when we need to say, "It's our time, we're getting in"?

Women's Language

On December 18, 2019, seven Democratic presidential candidates engaged in a nationally televised debate. Moderator and journalist Judy Woodruff closed the evening with a question that was meant to be in keeping with the "spirit of the season." She asked each of the candidates—two women and five men—if there was a fellow candidate to whom they'd like to either ask for forgiveness for some offense or give a gift. The peculiar question bewildered viewers and candidates alike.

After letting out a confused laugh, businessman Andrew Yang answered first, saying, "I don't think I have much to ask forgiveness for. You all can correct me on this." He then went on to describe his book and say he'd love to give all the candidates a copy and proceeded to pitch it to viewers, as well.

Mayor Pete Buttigieg followed his lead, also plugging his book. Then former Vice President Joe Biden said he'd give the gift of "making people's lives better." Senator Bernie Sanders mentioned his four books and said his gift would be the realization of his vision. Billionaire Tom Steyer promised the "gift of teamwork."

Only two candidates on that stage asked for forgiveness.

"I will ask for forgiveness," Senator Elizabeth Warren said. "I know that sometimes, I get really worked up, and sometimes I get a little hot. I don't really mean to."

"Well, I'd ask for forgiveness, anytime any of you get mad at me," Senator Amy Klobuchar said. "I can be blunt. But I am doing this because I think it is so important to pick the right candidate here."

In short, the men decided to give the gift of themselves, and the women asked for forgiveness. Their answers did not surprise me. While I cannot know what was going through their minds,

I would bet good money it did not occur to any of the men to apologize, let alone for getting "worked up" or being direct. I am certain Senators Warren and Klobuchar made a strategic play to appease the many women and men who may have been turned off by their demonstrations of anger or assertiveness. When they asked for forgiveness for stepping beyond the bounds of culturally sanctioned femininity, they were using a linguistic pattern that Robin Lakoff identified as "women's language."

In her 1973 paper, "Language and Woman's Place," Lakoff examined how women's speaking patterns unconsciously preserve and entrench gender inequalities. Her descriptions of typical male-female interactions and norms in the 1970s conjure images from *Mad Men*, where men in gray suits drank together and told off-color jokes in smoky bars but changed their tone and demeanor when "ladies" were present. Lakoff described a culture where women were meant to be arbiters of morality, protectors of polite society, and unwavering upholders of manners. This created linguistic norms where women used polite, proper, and grammatically exacting language.

Language, then, kept women in "their place."

When in the presence of women, men curbed their coarser language, slang, or swear words and mirrored women's formality in a so-called sign of respect to these pillars of virtue and decorum. Lakoff argued that the linguistic patterns of both women and men served to confine women and relegate them to a stifling role as exemplars of a patriarchy-defined morality, whether they wanted it or not.[5]

In the 1970s, many women were offended by Lakoff's argument. They took issue with her suggestion that the differences in women's and men's language were oppressive to women. They were taught that these differences favored women by exalting them as morally superior to men. While women's role as morally superior to men held certain benefits in certain circumstances, Lakoff was convinced it denied women the innumerable benefits of being a whole person, free from gender norms, misogyny, and stereotypes. She rejected the idea that treating women with genteel politeness was harmless flattery. It was, in Lakoff's view, a confining condescension that doubled down on the belief that women were ultimately subordinate and of little value in society. Thus, the role of the morally upright, eternally polite woman was a Trojan horse that actually precluded women from challenging their assigned roles and opposing the patriarchy. Language, then, kept women in "their place."

In her paper, Lakoff listed nine characteristics of women's language, which were the linguistic patterns she observed women use—some of which were a function of the pressure to be polite, and some of which were the result. Lakoff believed that polite society taught women to be tentative, hesitant, or even apologetic when speaking, as any speech that is too assured or assertive could upset others, upset a delicate social balance, or appear unseemly. Lakoff also noticed that to counterbalance an assertive speaking style, women habitually used what she called linguistic "forms," such as "tag questions" ("It's too late to go out, *isn't it*?") or "hedges" ("*I think* it's too late to go out").

Lakoff acknowledged that the "forms" themselves are neutral, and their meaning is derived from the context of their use. In certain cases, they can be intentionally deferential and collaborative where building consensus is advantageous. In other cases, they can be compassionate and protect feelings where hurt feelings would be needless or cruel. In yet other cases, they can protect us from retaliation or harm. Despite Lakoff's frustration with how women's language can inhibit women and reinforce their inferiority, she appreciates its constructive use in preserving safety or winning and maintaining social acceptance in certain cases—no small things, especially when considered in the context of cultures past and present where women's lives, livelihoods, or bodies could be under very real threat if they broke the rules of womanhood.

Lakoff takes issue with women's language when it is used in contexts where it serves no beneficial end to the woman. In such scenarios, women's language undercuts women's confidence, conviction, clarity, or intentions. When direct and assertive language poses no risk of offense or damage and a woman hedges or tags her language anyway, Lakoff says this amounts to an apology for merely speaking at all.

Ultimately, Lakoff believes that women's language is a marker of social ills—a symptom, but not the disease itself. She was among the first to trace social inequality to how women and men speak. She believed conversational expectations maintained a gender status quo and could subtly reinforce misogynistic norms and women's lack of options. With her game-changing paper, Lakoff sounded the alarm that, through the unconscious and habitual use of women's typical linguistic forms, women were unwittingly playing a role in their ongoing suppression and denigration. And so deep-seated in women's language are these patterns that they showed up—with both great irony and little surprise—on a presidential debate stage in 2019.

The Heart of the Matter

While Lakoff focused her linguistic analysis on gendered communication in society at large, Deborah Tannen focused her analysis on language in the workplace. In *Talking From 9 to 5*, Tannen recounts the story of a multinational corporation division head who asked managers to assess the performance of select members of their groups, which included both women and men, who were being considered for promotion.[6] Every single manager was a man, and every single one recommended men for promotion. All the managers cited a lack of confidence as the reason they did not recommend women. The division head rightly grew suspicious, since this group of women had all performed well enough to be considered for promotion. How was it possible that every single woman lacked confidence? Tannen's research revealed that managers perceived the women as lacking confidence partly because they did not see them as communicating and speaking with authority.

In Tannen's view, the way women tend to talk can be alien to men. So conditioned are boys in their same-sex playgroups to speak to establish or reinforce power dynamics within the hierarchy that, as men, they intuitively grasp the importance of this approach in a corporate setting. According to a 2014 paper from the Kelley School of Business at Indiana University, men learn to mimic the communication styles of more senior men. The men in the study understood that to be perceived as worthy of a senior position, they would have to act and talk with the same seniority as those with more hierarchical status.[7] Thus, when men see a woman speaking with a collaborative conversational style, many will perceive her as failing to speak with authority or project high status. Instead, they see a person who lacks confidence and is therefore not qualified for more seniority or power.

Therein lies the problem for women who want to advance in their careers, negotiate for promotions and pay raises, expand the scope of their responsibilities, or unapologetically demonstrate their confidence and executive presence. Corporations today were predominantly founded by and remain predominantly run by men. Thus, the rules of engagement were and still are set by men. It is a world where men usually evaluate our performance and decide whether or not we can advance. And men work and communicate in a world of hierarchy.

> **In order to operate and be perceived as leaders, women have to pull from conversational styles that have been denied us and feel foreign to us.**

Furthermore, because of the symbiotic relationship between men's conditioning and their historical grasp on power, men have been able to lay claim to the behaviors and communication styles of leadership. This means that in order to operate and be perceived as leaders, women have to pull from conversational styles that have been denied us and feel foreign to us. But the reality is—and the research shows—that communicating with the command of a leader is just as natural and available to women as it is to men.

When it comes to our professional lives, the immediate problem in front of women is this: Research has shown that people in positions of authority tend to like and respond positively toward communication styles that match their own.[8] So as long as men remain in the majority of authority positions, women who want to advance careers and realize ambitions must utilize language that addresses hierarchy and projects authority.

Our collaborative style will cease to appear inherently weak or always lacking confidence when women hold at least half of all senior and leadership roles. To get there, we must learn to avoid a collaborative style when it holds back our advancement and instead expand our style to include speech that is adapted to hierarchical dynamics. This becomes possible when we familiarize ourselves with the linguistic markers of a collaborative style and learn to remove them from our speech when they undermine our power, authority, and perception of confidence.

The Six Modifiers of Women's Conversational Style

In my many years of practice as a coach and teacher of corporate communication skills workshops, I have studied and identified the female linguistic patterns that most frequently hinder women's effectiveness and ultimately their advancement in the professional world. I repeatedly see the same handful of speech patterns that undermine women's desire or capacity to demonstrate their power and authority. I call them the six modifiers of women's conversational style. The common purpose of these modifiers is to "bubble wrap" the content of a woman's message so that it does not make others uncomfortable. Bubble wrapping smooths the sharp edges of a statement that might be too authoritative, assertive, decisive, or charged, and instead keeps a woman's language neutral and acceptable.

Lakoff rightly points out that these modifiers are neither good nor bad; they are neutral. In certain contexts, they can be leveraged to our benefit, and in others they can subvert our goals and ambitions. The problem arises when they become ingrained habits, such that they seep into almost all of our conversations without our conscious awareness. In my experience, our conditioning is so relentless that these modifiers have become habitual features in most women's speech. In professional settings where we must convey authority or conviction, the modifiers can switch from being useful to being harmful to us. They can offer protection where protection is not needed and can actually distort the perception of us as leaders. While certain professional scenarios do warrant a collaborative conversational style, exclusive reliance on such a style will eventually begin to hurt our career advancement.

The descriptions of the six modifiers of women's conversational style follow. To illustrate each, we will return to the swim story from the start of the chapter and imagine how each one sounds in a professional setting. Note that I'm defining these modifiers in terms of their detrimental effects when used in contexts that require leadership and a demonstration of confidence.

Modifiers can range from one word to multiple words throughout a sentence. It's also possible for sentences to include multiple modifiers. In the examples below, modifiers specific to the category are indicated in italics.

The six modifiers of women's conversation style, in terms to their detrimental effects to leaders, are:

1) **Hedge:** Hedges dilute clarity, conviction, and the impact of the statement. They employ non-absolute language as a way of removing strength or bluntness from statements.

Swim story: *"I hate to say it*, but *I think* it is our time to get in the pool."
Workplace: *"I hope* my data is comprehensive enough to be convincing."

2) **Tag question:** Tag questions turn an assertion into a question. They imply you are looking for approval or validation.
Swim story: "You are about to jump out, *right?*"
Workplace: "It would be better to go with a low-risk strategy, *wouldn't you agree?*"

3) **Indirect request:** These avoid conflict, preserve a relationship, or minimize power or status differences by lowering your status relative to the listener.
Swim story: *"Do you know* what time it is?"
Workplace: *"If you feel up to it*, I know a lot about this subject and *I wouldn't mind* being part of the meeting."

4) **Over-apologize:** Being overly apologetic allows one to politely state or ask for something without offending, inconveniencing, or imposing. Unnecessary apology diminishes status and can be perceived as a lack of confidence or conviction.
Swim story: *"I am so sorry to have to ask you to* get out."
Workplace: *"I am sorry if this offends anyone, and I feel bad that I have to say it*, but this could be a costly mistake."

5) **Qualify:** Qualifications dilute authority by infusing doubt into speech in order to create room for another's opinion or interpretation.

Swim story: *"I could be wrong,* but I think we have all lanes reserved at this time."

Workplace: *"Dave may know more about this than I do,* but I think it is correct to assume we can meet that time frame."

6) **Overly emphatic:** Strong or superfluous language can be interpreted as covering up for uncertainty or as overly emotional and therefore less credible.

Swim story: *"I know you are going to be annoyed with me for doing this,* but I really have to ask you to get out."

Workplace: *"I know I have said this before and you are probably sick of it, but I could not live with myself if this report is not perfect.* We really need to address some of the discrepancies."

Our work is to become mindful of these modifiers so that we can choose when to use or not use them, as opposed to using them unconsciously. They are not fixed. With intention and practice, they can be replaced with a new style of speaking that serves our goals.

Conscious Conversation

In 2014, the Gallup research organization found that workers with female managers were more likely than those with male managers to agree with such statements as "At work, my opinion seems to count" or "There is someone at work who encourages my development." In other words, employees with female managers report being more engaged in their work than those with male managers.[9]

Given what we know about conversational styles, we can see

how women's conditioning leaves us better prepared to manage compared to men. Whereas male managers are more likely to interact with their teams in ways that maintain hierarchy, women tend to interact with those they manage in ways that create collaboration and egalitarianism. Without a reflex to preserve hierarchy, women can be more nurturing of their team members' growth and development and more open to their opinions and ideas—often with the express purpose of grooming them to gain status. The modifiers women use to achieve a collaborative conversational style can be an asset when developing others' skills and encouraging others to weigh in and contribute. Yet, like any asset, they can become detrimental if used in the wrong context.

If one is a leader, inviting the opinions of everyone on the team can undermine perceived authority. If one is a leader, engaging in a lengthy, collaborative conversation can slow decisions when swift action is needed. This is where men's instinct to preserve hierarchy becomes a boon. People want leadership from leaders. They want their leaders to be decisive and have vision, clarity, and confidence in their convictions. When leaders cede too much of their authority to others, they can appear uncertain, create ambiguity, and lose the confidence of their teams.

The language style of managers and the language style of leaders is necessarily different. When one is inappropriately used in the context of the other, both the management and leadership can suffer.

My client Diana learned this the hard way. She accepted the role of director of human resources at a start-up, which marked her leap from management to senior leadership. Up to that point, two men on the leadership team had been functioning as the HR leads. In her first weeks, they paid extra attention to her performance to assess if she'd be as effective as they had been in the job. In a meeting with the leadership team, she mentioned that she was planning to take a few offices offline for a week to conduct recruiting interviews. Someone in the meeting asked her which offices she wanted to claim for the interviews, to which Diana responded, "I think I'll ask my team and get back to you."

The fact that she did not have an answer of her own and wanted to consult with her team led one of the former de facto HR men to say, "Why don't you just decide?"

As she recounted this story, I knew what the men in the room were thinking and what they would say before she told me. Diana was new to the team and wanted to honor their familiarity with the offices. She was also new to senior leadership. Having not yet consciously shifted her mindset and communication style to her new context, she was still defaulting to the collaborative style that had served her well up to this point. And, of course, the men on the leadership team wanted to know she could be decisive and trust in her own decisions. When she wasn't, they took it as weakness and challenged her.

There is a time and a place for leaders to solicit feedback from their teams. This was not one. It was a low-stakes, inconsequential decision. Had Diana made the decision then and there in the meeting, she could have easily fixed a mistake later if her team noted a conflict. Because of all the factors at play, Diana missed an early opportunity to signal to the team that she was a leader and that she had what it takes to sit at that table with them as a peer.

Diana had all the competence, skills, and experience to make a strong leader. But she needed to change her speaking style in order to change the power dynamic between herself and her peers. She needed to speak like a leader. As we talked through how she could have reacted differently in that instance, I presented her with two options:

Option 1: "I'm planning for us to take rooms 6, 7, and 8."

Option 2: "I'm planning for us to take rooms 6, 7, and 8. I'll confirm with my team and let you know if there is something I'm not aware of that would change this plan."

Why favor one option over the other? It depends on the audience and the context. An effective leader develops a skill for adapting conversational style to the person or people in the room and the important contextual considerations. When communicating an opinion, idea, or decision, it will be most effectively heard if tailored to the audience's priorities and values.

If Diana was in a room with senior men, I would suggest she go for option 1, as it is more decisive and in keeping with an "alpha" style. If there was a mix of women and men, option 2 could be more impactful. In option 2, Diana's intention to take certain rooms offline is clear and direct. Yet a second sentence is added to signal her newness at the company and lack of familiarity with protocols without sacrificing her decisiveness in the moment.

In order for Diana to choose the best option, I explained to her, she would have to step into the shoes of those in her audience in order to understand what drives them and what they value. One of the gifts of our conditioning is that women develop a deep capacity for empathy. When we must read the room and consciously discern the appropriate conversational style to advance our goals, our empathy becomes one of our greatest assets.

Becoming an Alpha Female

When women become adept at tweaking communication to resonate with an audience, they are functioning not like men but like alpha females, according to British professor and sociolinguist Judith Baxter, who studied the communication patterns of successful female leaders. In a 2013 article for *The Guardian*, she wrote that alpha females are successful because they are "embracing the masculine while skillfully preserving their identities as women," and they "judiciously draw on both masculine and feminine styles of language to create the right impact with their teams." Baxter describes the selection of language as pulling from a full "linguistic repertoire" and quotes a female leader who explains what utilizing all the tools in the repertoire looks like in practice: "I need to sound rather more assertive here, back off a little there. Draw this colleague out; put that colleague back in his place; it's a constant juggling act."[10]

In other words, alpha females know how to "thread the needle" with their linguistic choices—they toggle between a collaborative speaking style and an authoritative speaking style. They speak intentionally to achieve the power dynamic they

> In other words, alpha females know how to "thread the needle" with their linguistic choices—they toggle between a collaborative speaking style and an authoritative speaking style.

want in a room or with a person. They understand that being able to demonstrate leadership is a must if they are to command respect as leaders. And they also understand that being too commanding or too authoritative can risk penalty for disrupting the status quo. So they develop an instinct for identifying the appropriate mix of authoritative speaking style and collaborative speaking style—landing on a combination that will advance their agendas. Importantly, alpha females know not to discard their collaborative style; their aim is not to "act like a man" but pull from the most effective conversational styles typically used by both women and men based on the matter at hand.

Men have also begun to get this memo. According to Baxter, male leaders are beginning to embrace more stereotypically feminine behavioral tactics and a more empathetic conversational style in certain scenarios. In turn, these male leaders are speaking with a broader linguistic repertoire. Baxter believes this is because more and more men are appreciating the importance and power of emotional intelligence at the leadership level. But, Baxter asserts decisively: "…alpha women now have the edge because they constantly think about how they speak."[11]

The contradiction between our conditioning and our ambitions means that, unlike men, we've had to question how best to navigate the workplace for as long as we've been in it. As Baxter suggests, this makes us uniquely prepared to advance in a professional world that is increasingly demanding more thoughtful, nuanced conversation and leadership. Alpha women, who "constantly think about how they speak," have a great asset. We unlock and optimize our advantages, though, only when we become fully aware of our conditioning and the superpowers and deficits we have as a result. When we understand our conditioning and see it for what it is, rather than unconsciously remain under its influence, then we can take back the reins. We can reclaim our wholeness and step fully into the central agency of our lives. We can successfully act on our ambitions without scaling them back or leaving them behind. We can realize our dreams.

First, we must change our language.

CHAPTER 5

Reclaiming Our Power and Ambition

My client Erica was a senior director of operational strategy who provided strategic planning to company executives. Once a quarter, she met with a group of senior vice presidents to review the work her team had provided them. Since her interactions with this group were confined to this quarterly event, she had few opportunities to gain visibility and nurture relationships with them. Her direct report, Sabine, was closer to the actual work and therefore had stronger relationships with some of the SVPs in the group.

In one of our sessions, Erica told me about a recent event with Sabine. Erica had directed Sabine to schedule a joint meeting for the two of them and one of the SVPs. Developing a stronger relationship with each SVP was one of Erica's goals and part of her development plan for a promotion to vice president. When Erica had not received confirmation from Sabine that she'd scheduled the meeting, she asked Sabine for an update. Then she asked again. And then a third time.

Sabine's evasive behavior and lack of updates was causing Erica to feel paranoid. Her suspicions were soon validated when she learned that Sabine had held the meeting with the SVP without Erica and without informing her! When Erica recounted the events to me, she also shared two other instances where Sabine had intentionally cut Erica out of meetings.

I was taken aback by the description of Sabine's behavior and her brazen disrespect for Erica. What Sabine was doing was shockingly insubordinate and should raise the ire of any reasonable manager. I asked Erica how this made her feel, and she replied: "I am uncomfortable with it."

In merely *hearing* the story, I found myself angry about Sabine's behavior. In our previous sessions, Erica and I had strategized ways that she could deepen her relationships with the SVPs. I knew how critical this was to her, and I had a hard time believing that her reaction to Sabine's behavior was limited to discomfort. So I explored more with her about this series of events. Eventually, she admitted that she was "angry" with Sabine. But, she said, "uncomfortable" was the accurate description of how she felt about the prospect of telling Sabine she was angry with her.

Erica grew up in a home that demanded all women in her family be polite. She was constantly reminded to be considerate of others and behave courteously to everyone. Her classically "feminine" upbringing taught her only one way to engage with others. To accommodate her conditioning, Erica learned to disconnect herself from her more unpleasant feelings, as she had no way to give them voice or act on them without upsetting others. In turn, her ability to feel and articulate entire categories of feelings had been stunted. With politeness as her only option, Erica struggled to access the anger she felt in response to Sabine's provocative behavior. She also couldn't find the language to confront Sabine that would ensure Sabine would not act inappropriately again.

When I asked Erica how she planned to handle the situation, she said, "I think I'll tell Sabine that I was surprised by her actions."

With that, it was evident that she and I had some work to do. The word Erica would choose to characterize her emotion for this critical statement to Sabine had to achieve a few key goals. It had to be clear and authentic and leave Sabine with no uncertainty as to where she or Erica stood. The word "surprised" might be appropriate for a coworker with a track record of punctuality who showed up late to work one day without explanation. But Sabine's behavior was blatantly self-serving and inappropriate, making the word "surprised" inadequate. It did not align with the power dynamic that needed to be corrected between the two of them. Since Erica was at a loss for words to express her anger in a constructive fashion, we decided to write a script for her conversation with Sabine.

Writing a Script

Strategic script writing is a powerful tool for women who are ready to restore and expand their language repertoire. Beginning to use language from the assertive side of a full repertoire can feel uncomfortable and unnatural to many women at first. To ease some of this discomfort, I always recommend writing a script for important conversations. Scripts allow for experimentation, trial and error, and practice. They provide a structure for speaking so you feel more confident in what you are saying and don't get lost in nerves or what might be an emotional moment. Through the process of drafting a script—which you'll learn how to do in Part Two—women can literally find their voice.

In order for Erica's script to be effective, we needed to identify Sabine's *interests* and *goals*. Getting ahead was very important to Sabine, and Erica appreciated that her ambition translated into good and efficient work.

From there, we had to articulate the *outcome* she wanted from her conversation with Sabine. Erica's goal, she told me, was for Sabine to stop going behind her back to meet with SVPs. She also wanted Sabine simply to do what was asked of her at the first request. Erica knew that whatever she ended up saying to Sabine, she did not want to demotivate her or squash her ambition.

Next we had to consider the *context*. Because Erica had an aversion to "negative" or "aggressive" language, it was possible that her attempts up to this point to convey her mounting concern and frustration over Sabine's behaviors had not transmitted clearly to Sabine. Also, the working relationships Sabine had with the SVPs blurred the boundaries of hierarchy; Erica was more senior than Sabine, but Sabine had stronger relationships with people even more senior than Erica. Erica had not clarified her expectations about how they would approach these blurred boundaries, leaving them open to Sabine's exploitation. To reverse this pattern, Erica needed to project her seniority and the seriousness of her expectation that Sabine stop her behavior immediately.

Finally, we needed to determine the *strategy* for the type of language that would be most likely to help Erica achieve her goal amid the circumstances. Because Erica did not want to demotivate Sabine, she decided she did not want to come across as angry. Instead, she wanted to appear firm in her conviction that

Sabine's behavior was inappropriate and that she must abide by different expectations going forward. While we agreed that the word "surprised" had no place in her script, neither did the word "angry." Instead, we chose a mix of collaborative and assertive language, weaved together to communicate the seriousness of the situation without sounding angry.

We were now ready to write the script. We opened with a clear *headline* statement that articulated how Erica felt upon discovering Sabine's multiple instances of planning meetings with the SVPs alone. She landed on this: "I felt disrespected and frustrated to learn that you had repeatedly ignored my requests and scheduled a meeting with Javier without me. I want you to know that such behavior can't continue and understand why." To balance what might sound like a single attribution of blame, Erica then took some responsibility for not communicating clearly enough about the meetings and what she expected of Sabine in situations where there were blurred boundaries. Then, in no uncertain terms, Erica stated that she wanted Sabine to stop this behavior today.

Next, to *explain* why Sabine's behaviors were so upsetting to Erica, she clarified that the meetings with individual SVPs were her way of signaling her investment in their work, success, and larger business objectives. We made clear that Sabine's actions directly undermine those goals.

Lastly, to *support* her overall point, Erica recounted the specific instances she knew of when Sabine scheduled her own meetings with SVPs and failed to update Erica on the meetings Sabine did schedule. Erica also stated her clear expectation that Sabine heed her requests the first time they are made and that a failure to comply would have consequences.

Erica met with Sabine a few days later and delivered her script. After the meeting, she emailed to let me know how it went. She wrote: "Overall, it went well. I think I made my point with the right tone. I am sure she was somewhat 'surprised' because she has never seen me communicate in this way before. I suspect there will need to be more meetings like this to reinforce my expectations and my authority."

While reinforcement would be needed, Erica had righted the ship. With her carefully chosen, decisive, yet supportive language, she had established the power dynamic she wanted with Sabine. She had also taken her first step in the work of growing ever more comfortable speaking and behaving assertively and without apology.

The Cultural Sieve

Over the next few months, Erica and I went through several scripting exercises. With each script, new language would come a little more readily to her. Over time, she grew more adept at writing her own scripts, which she now always does in advance of high-stakes or uncomfortable conversations. Every time she engages in such conversations, she gains that much more confidence in herself.

She also learned to break her habit of politeness. While being polite can be a good strategy in certain circumstances, it is no longer Erica's default. Before responding, she has learned to pause, get clear on her goals, and then adapt her language and style for the context and audience. Her new awareness of her conditioning has helped restore her sense of agency and authenticity. It has put her in control of her language rather than at the mercy of old habits. Now when she's polite, it's because she's *choosing* to be polite after deciding that doing so will work for, not against, her. Put another way, she is mastering the art of making conscious choices about what she says and how she says it.

Erica was also relieved to find that she was growing comfortable with her seniority. The ability to project authority had always eluded her. She held a belief that she didn't need to assert her authority. It just "wasn't her style," she would say. She doesn't like to create conflict, she would explain, and to her it was impossible to have authority without conflict. But her experience with Sabine exposed Erica to the kinds of conflicts that can arise in the absence of authority and when collaboration is prioritized over hierarchy. She now appreciated that part of being a leader is asserting authority in an effective way and at the right time. She understood that she had to use language that conveyed and reinforced the appropriate power dynamic in every conversation.

> Language is one of the most consequential expressions of our cultural conditioning.

Because Erica was learning to use a full language repertoire, she began uncovering new feelings. Buried under the blanket of politeness were feelings of irritation, frustration, anger, and even competitiveness. By rediscovering these aspects of herself, she found that the language for these feelings was now within her reach.

Sentence by sentence and choice by choice, Erica changed her language and chipped away at her conditioning. The impact on her career was significant. She grew more visible to senior-level stakeholders as she sought and received recognition for her work. Eventually, she won the promotion she had wanted.

Language is one of the most consequential expressions of our cultural conditioning. Before women even get to the point of speaking, what we intend to say is filtered through a cultural sieve of "feminine" expectations, where all of our thoughts, feelings, reactions, wants, needs, ideas, preferences, and beliefs are processed through the three constraints. The constraints strip out any emotion that is unpleasant to others. They dilute or even remove our assertiveness and the potential to offend. They separate us from using all the modes of communication at our disposal to make points with conviction, command, or even force. For women of color, there can exist a second sieve that further filters the self through biases and discriminatory perceptions.

The sieve leaves behind language that has departed, sometimes starkly, from our original intent. What's left is only a partial representation of our real selves, ambitions, or ideas. What's left is an attempt to be Considerate, Contained, and Collaborative all the time, even when it can work against us.

What's left is "surprised," when really we are furious.

Reclaiming Our Full Language Repertoire

The work of identifying and overriding the effect of the cultural sieve so that we can enjoy our authentic selves is vital. It can radically change our relationship to others and ourselves. It can change how we perceive and conduct ourselves in all areas of our lives, not just in our careers. It can heal wounds and create a sense of optimism and possibility. It is the kind of consciousness-raising that requires introspection, self-analysis, and dedication. It is also the kind of work that often requires a lot of time.

But if you want to grow your professional opportunities now, taking charge of your career cannot wait for you to do intensive, long-term work. Opportunities for more exposure and power will pass you by.

To help clients meet their professional goals, I focus on changing their language. Changing our language is a version of "fake it until you make it." After working with the resources and script formats I share with clients—which I provide for you in Part Two—to help them make new language choices from a full repertoire, clients repeatedly tell me they feel liberated. They feel enormous relief from saying statements like "You've been promising me this promotion for eight months. If you cannot say with certainty that I will be put up in the next promotion cycle, I have to seriously consider whether there is a future here for me" instead of asking, "When do you think you'll know if I'm going to be put up for promotion in the next cycle?" Or using direct language, such as "With my track record and institutional knowledge, I am the most qualified candidate for the role" instead of "I think I could do the job, even if I don't have every qualification on the list." Over time, women find that they no longer reflexively diminish the impact of their statements. Instead, speaking assertively becomes their default option, and modified collaborative language becomes an option to leverage when strategically advantageous for their goals. Having liberated

> Having liberated themselves from self-limiting language habits, women feel empowered.

themselves from self-limiting language habits, women feel empowered.

They also begin to feel different. Choosing, practicing, and speaking new language rewires our brain. Old assumptions and behaviors are challenged. More opportunities for expression of our authentic selves feel available. Women find themselves growing more comfortable un-containing their bodies, taking up more space when they speak, using more vocal range, and communicating with more confidence and conviction. They find they have the courage to take some calculated risks and see them pay off—literally and figuratively. Ultimately, they find that they are becoming alpha females.

> With consistent use of a full language repertoire, you will find that you yourself are different. You will discover that you have grown into an unabashed, unapologetic, and powerful "tall poppy."

Sometimes the discomfort with speaking from a full repertoire can linger as you start this work. Even the most self-assured women tell me they feel some anxiety before a conversation where they must be direct and unyielding. Clients ranging from executives to managers have called me before going into a difficult meeting, where they would deliver one of our scripts, to tell me they're nervous. Typically, these women express doubt that they can stick to the script as we designed it. I remind them that, because we have already practiced the script multiple times, what they need to say exists in their muscle memory. All they have to do is trust that, when the moment comes, their preparation will take over. They may stumble here or there, and that is OK. They don't have to be perfect, I remind them, they just have to be clear. Lastly, I tell them to take a deep breath.

This, too, is your charge. You don't have to change how uncomfortable it might initially feel to speak from a full language repertoire. You simply have to tolerate it. You can learn to feel discomfort while also confidently pushing forward with your plan. You can learn to let discomfort simply exist in you without distracting from your larger goal.

Expect that you will make mistakes, or stumble, or wish you had chosen this word instead of that word. Do not let mistakes or setbacks cause you to back down from your ambitions. Your eyes are now open to how backing down in the past may have stalled your career, resulted in missed opportunities, left money on the table, or simply prevented you from saying what you really wanted to say. The costs of giving into your fears and adhering to your conditioned and limited language are too high. The potential rewards of persisting as you reclaim your language are too great to miss any longer.

The more you make conscious choices about the words you speak, the more credibility and respect you will gain. In time, you will see more of your goals met and ambitions realized. You will find that people are responding to you differently. With consistent use of a full language repertoire, you will find that you yourself are different. You will discover that you have grown into an unabashed, unapologetic, and powerful "tall poppy"—with great, big ambitions *and* the wherewithal to act on them.

In time, you will find that you are a woman who can use language to own, assert, and enjoy her power.

PART TWO

Finding Our Language

Resources for Utilizing a Full
Language Repertoire

A Note on Part Two

As professional women, we gain numerous benefits by learning how to communicate from a full language repertoire. In addition to discovering new and powerful parts of ourselves, there are material advantages to be gained as well.

A 2017 study from labor economists in Europe analyzed female and male professionals to determine how demonstrating more stereotypically masculine traits affected the careers of female employees. The stereotypically masculine traits included being strong, technically competent, ambitious, self-sufficient, authoritative, and in control of emotions. The stereotypically feminine traits included being empathetic, sensitive, loyal, and caring. Researchers found that women who exhibited so-called "masculine" traits were more likely to win access to typically male-dominated occupations. They were also more likely to earn up to 10 percent higher wages than women who demonstrated only "feminine" traits.[1]

While I do not prefer the characterization of any trait as strictly masculine or feminine, such perceptions still dominate our workplaces. When we adhere only to so-called "feminine" traits, we risk being overlooked for advancement and more pay.

In the following chapters, I provide a series of resources to help you counter your "feminine" conditioning and replace it with more powerful language and action. These resources will help you speak with directness and confidence; assert your needs and your ideas effectively; achieve the right balance of power with coworkers; and embody an authoritative presence that can propel your career.

The resources I share in Part Two are the same ones I provide to clients and those who attend my *Women, Language, and Power* workshops. They are designed to be simple, easy to use, and very effective. Over time, they will create a mindset shift, such that the structures and best practices that follow become a reflex.

CHAPTER 6
Choosing Language That Advances Your Goals

When marketers craft a message to sell a product, their first rule is to position the product in terms of the value it will create for the customer. To do this, they use language that the customer would use so that the message resonates with them, feels relevant to them, and compels them to make a purchase.

Leaders intuitively do something similar. They understand that a central feature of being an effective leader is success-fully influencing others. They know that their capacity to influence is a function of how skillfully they can tailor messages to the needs, values, concerns, or aspirations of those in a given audience. Such tailoring requires that leaders take into account rele-vant circumstances or factors. From there, they craft messages most likely to be received positively by the audience. If you want to be a leader, this is a skill you must master.

> To "thread the needle"—that is, to find just the right mix of assertive and collaborative language that will help us achieve our goals—we must draw from a full language repertoire.

Yet, for women, there is an additional consideration. When we tailor messages to audiences, we also have to assess how assertive our language needs to be in order to advance our goals. As you know, if we are too assertive, we can be perceived as aggressive, pushy, or dominant. But if we fail to be assertive enough, we can be perceived as passive, cautious, or unconvincing. To "thread the needle"—that is, to find just the right mix of assertive and collaborative language that will help us achieve our goals—we must draw from a full language repertoire.

A full language repertoire includes everything from the assertive and direct language that our conditioning has denied us to highly collaborative language. It also includes the different ways we can deliver our message, like tone of voice, volume, body language, and nonverbal cues (all of which I address in Chapter 10).

> **Initially, making new language choices may feel clumsy and uncomfortable. This is why planning in advance is so powerful.**

Many women do not feel a full language repertoire is available to them and instead over-rely on a collaborative conversational style by default. To help replace this habit with a more conscious and intentional use of a full language repertoire, I advise women to write down what they want to say before going into critical conversations—as I did with Erica in Chapter 5.

Initially, making new language choices may feel clumsy and uncomfortable. This is why planning in advance is so powerful—it allows you to practice using assertive language. It protects you from falling into unconscious language habits that could undermine your goal. The more you practice new and unfamiliar language, the more confident and comfortable you will become with it. In time, you will rely less on the collaborative conversational style by default and more on an expansive language repertoire by conscious choice. Like Judith Baxter's alpha females, we can use assertive language to push forward a little here and use collaborative language to pull back a little there—with the ultimate intention of delivering a message most resonant and appealing to the audience and designed to achieve our goals.

How to Identify the Language Mix That Will Achieve Your Goal

Before you go into critical conversations, taking the time to consider the dynamics and identify the mix of assertive and collaborative language you want to use will help you achieve your goal. To that end, I provide a series of five prompts to determine the language that is most appropriate given the audience, the context, and what you hope to achieve.

Ultimately, the prompts will prepare you to write a script. I call the prompts "the Foundational Five," as these five key questions help you think through your goal, approach, and some of the specific language you want to include in your script. The nature of the conversation you are planning to have will dictate the length and detail of the script you need. A script can range from a set of bullet points to a long-form document in which you write every word you intend to say. It can be four sentences or four paragraphs, depending on how necessary it is for you to plan exactly what you will say. While some clients will come close to memorizing their scripts for certain situations, they don't need to be recited word for word. The point of scripting is to prevent you from going into important conversations unprepared.

The Foundational Five inform the planning of conversations and presentations that I will address in the following chapters. As

I introduce you to the Foundational Five below, I also provide an example for each prompt to bring clarity and showcase how they prepare you to write a script. In these examples, the person writing the script is an employee with a new manager who is micromanaging her work. She understands his need to remain informed and involved, but she wants to find more effective ways to work with him that give her more autonomy.

The Foundational Five

1) **Who is the audience, and what are their goals, priorities, or interests?**

   Example: My audience is my new manager, Reyn, and he cares about establishing both his authority and a good working relationship with me.

2) **What is your goal for the conversation?**

   This could be anything from expressing a feeling, communicating a decision, setting a boundary, asking for a promotion, etc.

   Example: My goal is to convince my manager that I have the project under control and that the face-to-face meetings he's demanding for updates slow down our progress. I want to agree on a more efficient process.

3) **What is the relevant context?**

   What circumstantial or relational issues influence your approach to the situation?

   Example: My manager has been in his new role for three months. He wants to feel involved and does not want to risk being uninformed. He doesn't trust me yet. I don't want to alienate him, but I need more autonomy.

4) What is your strategy?

The three strategy options are assertive, mixed (assertive/collaborative), or collaborative. Given the audience, goal, and context, what mix of language will be most effective? That is, how assertive should your language be? Is there a reason to include a mix of more collaborative language? Keep in mind that, at some point, using too much collaborative language can undermine your goal.

Example: I will need a mix of assertive and collaborative language. I want to be assertive about my ability to successfully manage the project. I also want to get his buy-in for alternatives to face-to-face meetings.

5) What are the most important sentences you want to assert clearly and without modifiers?

Write down the precise language you want to use to express your goal. This will help you avoid inadvertent collaborative modifiers in this language, which must remain assertive and clear. You may need one only sentence, depending on your situation.

Example: "I am fully confident this project will come in on time and within budget."

"I would like to determine a process for updating you that is as effective as face-to-face meetings but not dependent on them."

Write the Script

With your goal, your strategy, and the specific language you want to use to express your goal identified, you can turn to the script. You may feel that the Foundational Five have sufficiently prepared you to write a script, develop bullet points that sketch out what you want to cover, or something in between. Should you need additional scripting guidance, in the following three chapters I offer two formats and a framework for different speaking scenarios.

For our example here, we'll use a format I explain in detail in Chapter 7, the Headline-Explain-Support (HES) format. It is excellent for circumstances that require you to make an assertion concisely, convincingly, and with supporting evidence. For our purposes here, I'll use the HES format simply to show what a script for the new manager scenario could look like.

Example: Fully Written Script

Reyn, I want to bring you up to date on the website launch and agree on the most efficient way for you to stay informed on our progress. I am fully confident this project will come in on time and within budget. I want you to be confident of that as well. Therefore, I would like to determine a process for updating you that is as effective as face-to-face meetings but not dependent on them. In the last month, because of your schedule, we have had only two 30-minute meetings. When I have to wait two weeks for your input or sign-off on something, it slows down our decision-making and timelines by weeks. I would like to explore other ways I can give you updates and get more immediate feedback that isn't dependent on us being in the room together. I want you to feel you have a good grasp on our progress. If we can come to an agreement, I will update the team and we can start our new process next week.

Example: Bullet-Pointed Script
- I want to update you + agree on best way to update going forward
- I am fully confident this project will be on time and within budget
- I would like to determine a process for updating you that is as effective as face-to-face meetings
- Face-face slows decision-making and timelines
- What would work best?
- We can start next week

One Scenario, Three Language Options

To illustrate how language changes based on circumstantial dynamics, we'll adapt language for slightly different contexts in a scenario every woman knows all too well: being interrupted. Being interrupted is common for women; demanding that we get the floor back is not. When we fail to resume speaking our point, we lose out on opportunities to ensure that our thoughts, ideas, and needs are fully communicated and heard. Over time, these lost opportunities can have a material impact on our advancement.

With being interrupted as the example issue, I will fill in the prompts and then show three responses that exemplify different language choices based on different contextual circumstances.

Example:

1) **Who is the audience, and what are their goals, priorities, or interests?** Rachael wants to get her points heard quickly and isn't aware of the impact she is having by interrupting.

2) **What is your goal for the conversation?** To respectfully slow Rachael down and make her aware that she needs to let others speak and complete their thoughts.

3) **What is the relevant context?** The most relevant context is your level of seniority in relation to Rachael (which will change in each example for the purposes of being instructive).

4) **What is your strategy?** Each example will use one of the three strategies: assertive, mixed (assertive/collaborative), or collaborative.

5) **What is the most important sentence you want to preserve?** "I want to finish my point." (Remember: This is the core statement of your desired outcome and must remain free of modifiers.)

Strategy: **Assertive**

What is the relevant context? You and Rachael are peers. You can be straightforward, stop her, and finish your point.

Language: "Rachael, I want to finish my point."

Strategy: **Mixed (Assertive/Collaborative)**

What is the relevant context? You are a manager, and Rachael is a director. You have to be respectful to show some deference.

Language: "Rachael, I am curious to hear your opinion. But I want to finish my point first so you have a complete understanding of my position."

Strategy: **Collaborative**

What is the relevant context? You are a senior manager, and the meeting has a mix of your peers, senior directors, and Rachael, who is the only VP in the room.

Language: "Thank you, Rachael. I know you have questions. I want to finish my point and then answer any questions you have. Will that work?"

What to Keep in Mind When Planning and Practicing Language From a Full Repertoire

- I tell clients to draft as much language as they need in order to feel confident going into the conversation. When crafting my own scripts, I usually write the first few sentences word for word so I have a strong start. I then follow with a bullet-pointed list of everything I want to cover. For some points, I highlight specific words to make sure I use that exact phrasing. For others, I write down enough to know the point, but I don't worry about how I will say it. It is best to write out the most direct assertions explicitly to avoid any of the modifying language (hedging, qualifying, etc.) that can otherwise slip in out of habit.
- There's no one right mix of assertive and collaborative language and style. It always depends on your goal, the audience, and the context.

- The language you choose must ultimately account for the power dynamic you are trying to establish or reinforce. For example, are you trying to assert your authority? Remind someone you are of equal authority? Or make your conviction clear while also acknowledging the authority of the person to whom you're speaking?

- Make sure that the sentences articulating your goal are assertive. Surround these sentences with collaborative language as appropriate.

- We often find ourselves in situations where we must make real-time decisions about how assertive our language should be. I encourage you to have a number of pre-planned responses ready to go for such situations.

- Once you've drafted what you want to say, practice saying it out loud several times. For high-stakes conversations, record yourself practicing or practice in front of a trusted friend or colleague. For *really* high-stakes conversations or potentially career-advancing presentations, I go over my script in my head at every opportunity—while swimming, while in my car, while making dinner. The consequences of conversations and presentations exist on a spectrum of low to high. The more consequential the script, the more practice it warrants.

- As you practice out loud, consider the tone, emphasis, and body language you might want to use to achieve your goal.

- Lastly, while the Foundational Five are designed to help you plan key sentences or a script in advance of important conversations, they are also meant to help you develop a mindset—one where consciously choosing the language mix that will achieve your goal is a reflex. To help you cultivate this mindset, let these prompts be the backdrop against which you approach all critical professional conversations. Over time, you will find yourself relying less on the prompts and more on speaking from a full language repertoire as a matter of habit.

Your Turn: Stripping Out the Modifiers From Language

For many women, it can take practice to craft sentences free of modifiers. To that end, I provide a worksheet in my workshop on which I ask women to identify the particular modifier in a sentence. Once they've completed this step, they rewrite the sentence with no modifiers. Complete the exercise that follows, as I think you will find it to be eye-opening.

A Refresher: The Six Modifiers of Women's Conversational Style:

1) **Hedge:** Hedges dilute clarity, conviction, and the impact of the statement. They employ non-absolute language as a way of removing strength or bluntness from statements.

2) **Tag question:** Tag questions turn an assertion into a question. They imply you are looking for approval or validation.

3) **Indirect request:** These avoid conflict, preserve a relationship, or minimize power or status differences by lowering your status relative to the listener.

4) **Over-apologize:** Being overly apologetic allows one to politely state or ask for something without offending,

inconveniencing, or imposing. Unnecessary apology diminishes status and can be perceived as a lack of confidence or conviction.

5) **Qualify:** Qualifications dilute authority by infusing doubt into speech in order to create room for another's opinion or interpretation.

6) **Overly emphatic:** Strong or superfluous language can be interpreted as covering up for uncertainty or as overly emotional and therefore less credible.

Exercise

First, identify the collaborative conversation modifier used in each of the six sentences that follow. (Note that it's possible for a sentence to have more than one modifier.) Then write an assertive version of each sentence. Answers and suggested assertive sentences follow.

Example

Collaborative sentence: "We may need to rethink this approach. I am not sure it really covers what we need it to cover."

Modifier(s): Indirect request and hedge

Assertive sentence: "I want to rethink this approach. It is not comprehensive enough."

Your Turn

1) "I'm not sure we have enough materials."
   Modifier(s):
   Assertive sentence:

2) "I really appreciate your help because I could not have done this without you. Really, it was so nice of you."
Modifier(s):
Assertive sentence:

3) "David may know more about this than I do, but I think the data supports our conclusion to take action at this point."
Modifier(s):
Assertive sentence:

4) "Sorry, but I think I was next in line."
Modifier(s):
Assertive sentence:

5) "You agree, don't you, that our budget is too tight at this point to add anything?"
Modifier(s):
Assertive sentence:

6) "I don't want to be a bother, but if you have time to update the spreadsheet, I would really appreciate it."
Modifier:
Assertive sentence:

Answers

1) "I'm not sure we have enough materials."
Modifier(s): Hedge
Assertive sentence: "We do not have enough materials."

2) "I really appreciate your help because I could not have done this without you. Really, it was so nice of you."
Modifier(s): Overly emphatic
Assertive sentence: "I appreciate your help very much."

3) "David may know more about this than I do, but I think the data supports our conclusion to take action at this point."
Modifier(s): Qualify
Assertive sentence: "The data supports our conclusion to take action at this point."

4) "Sorry, but I think I was next in line."
Modifier(s): Over-apologize and hedge
Assertive sentence: "I was next in line."

5) "You agree, don't you, that our budget is too tight at this point to add anything?"
Modifier(s): Tag question
Assertive sentence: "The budget is too tight at this point to add anything to it."

6) "I don't want to be a bother, but if you have time to update the spreadsheet, I would really appreciate it."
Modifier(s): Indirect request
Assertive sentence: "Please update the spreadsheet."

Pushing Through Our Fear to Find Our Power

In our early days of crafting language for important conversations together, some of my female clients will express concern that the language is too assertive, or maybe even borders on aggressive. Their concern that the language is aggressive is typically due to a lack of familiarity with language free of modifiers. If you find yourself shying away from using assertive language, ask someone you trust to give you feedback on what you've written. I am confident that, in many cases, any fears that your assertive language is borderline aggressive will not be affirmed. However, having a second set of eyes or ears on your script can be helpful.

Women quickly discover relief in no longer having to modify so much of their language.

In my experience, women quickly discover relief in no longer having to modify so much of their language. Several of my clients have remarked that, when there is no reason to be particularly collaborative, they feel liberated in making their point in a straightforward, direct manner. They also comment that by speaking assertively more often, they are developing a new, more comfortable, and even enjoyable relationship with their own power. Just as they have experienced, you too will change your language and find your power.

CHAPTER 7

Making Effective Assertions

There's an expression in journalism: "Don't bury the lede." The "lede" is the introductory section of a news story. When done right, it includes the main idea, frames the reader's thinking and expectations for what's to come, and entices the reader to read on. Editors use the expression to remind reporters to introduce the most critical and captivating information immediately, rather than bury it further down in the story. The rest of the article is where writers can expand on the main idea and offer details and descriptions.

Outside of the newsroom, my experience has shown me that women are much more likely to bury the lede than men are. This is usually due to a tendency to give too much context too soon in a statement to avoid the discomfort of immediately and bluntly making the assertion. In professional settings, we encounter circumstances every day where we must be concise and to the point, or else we risk losing our audience.

When I began developing my *Women, Language, and Power* workshop, I created a scripting format to help women avoid burying the lede. The format organizes the assertion of an idea in a way that makes it concise and easy to follow. It also ensures that the main idea (or lede) is stated immediately and without modifiers. I call it the Headline-Explain-Support format, or

HES for short. It is a simple and effective format, derived from the "core message" framework I learned back when I was a coach at PowerSpeaking, Inc.

In 1985, Frederick Gilbert—author of *Speaking Up: Surviving Executive Presentations* and *How Ordinary People Can Make Extraordinary Presentations*—founded PowerSpeaking, a communications training company in Silicon Valley. His wife, Mary McGlynn, is the president and owner. They are considered pioneers in multiple types of communications—from executive to technical to sales and beyond. Their work centered on making presentations, and one of their signature concepts was the idea of identifying a "core message" for a presentation. The core message is a concise, bottom-line assertion that sums up the entire presentation and becomes a recall mechanism to help audiences remember the main idea, even days later. In the PowerSpeaking presentation skills workshops, participants are guided through the work of summarizing the core message as succinctly as possible and then building their presentations in support of it. When the need to help women avoid burying the lede in everyday work conversations became clear to me, I saw the opportunity to use an adaptation of PowerSpeaking's core message framework in the HES format.

What Is the HES Format?

The HES format starts with a clear and strong positional statement, or the *headline*. The headline answers the question, *What do I believe?* The answer gives listeners an immediate understanding of the speaker's position on a subject. When your audience leaves the room, it is the one thing from all you will have said that you want them to remember. It is a distilled version of everything you will then go on to explain. For example, if you asked me why so many people are afraid of public speaking, I might answer with the headline, "People are terrified of saying or doing something embarrassing that makes them feel exposed." Immediately, listeners have a sense of my position on why people avoid public speaking. And, importantly, they will also wonder why I hold this position and will want more information.

The second section of the format is the *explanation* of the headline. This is where the speaker details why she holds the position she does. The explanation answers the question, *Why do I believe my headline statement?* In our example of why people fear public speaking, the explanation would outline why people are so fearful of judgment that they avoid public speaking. Many speakers merge the explanation and the headline, which can dilute the impact of the headline. This is why the HES format separates the headline from the explanation—it allows listeners to really hear and consider the headline. Even if listeners get lost during the speaker's explanation, they can still grasp and retain the headline.

Once listeners understand the explanation, they naturally want data or information that validates what's been articulated up to this point. In the *support* section, the speaker outlines examples, data, or anecdotal experience to answer the question, *How can I validate my belief?* In addition to bringing credibility to the position, the support section helps women avoid the trap of being accused of using their feelings, rather than data or examples, to justify their positions.

How to Use the HES Format

When needing to make a direct, well-supported assertion—whether in a presentation to VPs or at an important meeting with your manager—the HES format will ensure you write a script that is both concise and appropriately detailed in validating your point. Before you fill out the format, think through the Foundational Five prompts outlined in Chapter 6 to inform your language choices in each of the three parts of the HES format. Explanation of the format is as follows:

The HES Format Answers Three Essential Questions:

Headline: What do I believe?
Explain: Why do I believe it?
Support: How can I validate it?

Headline: A headline is concise; aim for one sentence, and never let it be more than three sentences. If you find it's taking you more than three sentences to articulate your main point, this is typically a sign that you are already explaining it—which should be reserved for the next step. Avoid modifiers that will sabotage your efforts to articulate your headline as clearly as possible.

Example: "Our first priority is the identification of a set of core competencies that all managers will be expected to demonstrate."

153

Explanation: Your explanation should clarify what brought you to your conclusion, as expressed in the headline, on this subject. This section should cover a well-organized flow of one to three of your most convincing points that expand upon your headline. The points should build on one another to create a coherent explanation. Depending on how much your audience knows about the subject, you may need to start with some brief context or you may be able to dive right into your explanation.

Example: "Managers are the number one reason employees cite for leaving a company. Most of our managers have come into their roles through promotions within our company. Since we have not offered any learning and development programs, they have little to no formal training in management. We have a very high rate of attrition right now. One of our top company objectives is to reduce attrition. Starting with manager training is critical."

Support: The support section should provide objective validation for your main point. Support can include data, examples, and anecdotal experiences that bolster your argument. It is important to consider which type of supportive information will be most persuasive to your audience.

Example: "Of the 75 percent of employees in exit interviews who reference their manager as the top reason for their departure, their most common and specific criticisms of managers are a lack of development and feedback, clarity on goals and outcomes, and poor team management. In our company, 85 percent of our managers came to us out of college or with no previous management experience. As far as learning and development, we should invest where we have the most direct impact on employee retention."

After giving your HES statement, you may feel satisfied with how you made your point and move on. However, if checking for clarity or a response from the audience is important or wise, then I suggest leveraging the power of the pause. After completing your HES statement, simply pause for two to three seconds to see if anyone has an immediate response, like a signal of comprehension, a question, or a rebuttal. Many speakers do not pause to give the audience time to consider what they have just heard and offer a response. Both women and men tend to speak continuously until they are interrupted by someone interjecting or asking a question. A pause is a powerful way to demonstrate your confidence and authority, as well as to gauge the audience's response to what you said in your HES statement. Once your audience confirms understanding, you can move on.

How to Use the HES Format in Conversation
In a situation like a meeting, where dialogue must be efficient and to the point, the HES format might be all you need to make a strong and effective headline statement. But sometimes, specifically in a conversation, an expanded version of the HES is necessary to leave room for a more natural conversational flow without sacrificing the directness and thoughtful support of your assertion.

In Chapter 6, I provided an example of a script built from the HES format in which an employee needed to ask her manager for fewer face-to-face meetings, as they were slowing down project progress. In such a scenario, it would be unnatural to dive right into a headline. Before the HES, you might want to consider the relevant *context* that bears mentioning before articulating your headline. As you draft a brief opening to your conversation, consider what the audience already knows about the topic of your HES and what you must state explicitly so that your headline is contextualized for them. While it can be useful to briefly refresh your audience on a topic, stop short of providing information they already have.

The context sets you up to deliver the headline, explain, and support sections of your HES, after which you want to *engage* your audience. How much you engage them is a function of your goal and strategy. In some cases, it is to your advantage to build consensus or confirm buy-in at this point. Depending on your goal, you can give the person or people with whom you are speaking a chance to respond, ask a question, or seek additional explanation or support. Or you may want to direct the conversation in a certain way by asking a specific and pre-planned question, such as "Do you agree?" "Is your experience similar?" "Is there something you would add?" "What else do you think we need to consider?" or "Is there other information you need?"

And finally, take care to address *next steps*. Articulate and get confirmation on exactly what you want to happen moving forward. Often, next steps are vague, such as "Get back to me" versus "I will need an answer by Thursday before our 12 p.m.

meeting." Being specific makes it easy for the speaker to know if the audience can or will comply with her request or if they have questions about how to proceed. If next steps are vague, it can create miscommunication and confusion.

An example of the HES format expanded for conversation is as follows:

Context: "Bruce, we've had the senior program manager role open only to external candidates for six months. No one in the candidate pool we've interviewed has had both the skill set we need and the fit for this unique team."

Headline: "We need to move forward with an internal candidate. Given how behind the team is, we don't have the luxury of time to continue to look at unknown candidates."

Explain: "An internal candidate would be able to hit the ground running, as they would be familiar with the team, and we can provide help to fill the gaps of their experience."

Support: "This worked very well when the marketing team hired internally. Because of her work on the corporate communications team, Jenna was able to jump right in, begin meeting her goals, and played a key role in helping the marketing team meet and surpass benchmarks. Meanwhile, Robin mentored her closely in planning the first half of the year."

Engage: "From your perspective and given what I have laid

out, is there any reason we should continue to focus solely on internal candidates?"

Next Steps: "I would like to announce the open role next week and start interviewing the week after. If you agree, I will notify Asri to make the announcement and then begin scheduling interviews with a panel I've identified. Please confirm by Monday. Thank you."

The HES Format Expanded for Conversational Use

Context: What does your audience need to know to understand the headline?

Headline: What do I believe?

Explain: Why do I believe it?

Support: How can I validate it?

Engage: What kind of interaction do I want to encourage?

Next Steps: What needs to happen now?

What to Keep in Mind When Using the HES Format

In my experience, there are a few issues that women struggle with most when writing a script with the HES format. The first is crafting a headline that is as succinct as possible. The tendency to want to say too much or to modify strong assertions makes drafting a concise headline challenging. I could say, "It is not clear to me that asking for additional resources is worth the damage to our credibility. I am not sure we can afford that." Or I could say, "Asking for additional resources would damage our credibility. This is not a risk we should take." In length, conviction, and tone, these are two very different headline statements. I find that it can take a person two or three iterations to arrive at a headline that accurately captures what she wants to say and how she wants to say it. Iterating and improving is time well spent. Refine your headline as needed so that you deliver a powerful, concise headline that grabs your audience and conveys your confidence.

Second, many women struggle to pinpoint the ideal amount of information to include in the support section. This is usually a function of being too close to the content. As needed, test-run the support section with someone whose perspective can help you identify the appropriate information and how much you need to say.

Lastly, women are often accused of relying on their feelings to support their opinions, which can make their headline statements sound less convincing. Statements such as "I believe," "I feel strongly," "This feels like a good fit to me," or "It seemed that way to me" give audiences who want objective validation an easy reason to dismiss you and your ideas. Be on alert for such statements as you write your HES. For example, in the support section of our written HES example, I wrote, "Because of her work on the corporate communications team, Jenna was able to jump right in, begin meeting her goals, and played a key role in helping the marketing team meet and surpass benchmarks." Contrast this with "Jenna seemed to be pretty well prepared when she joined the marketing team." By relying on evidence of Jenna's success, the point moves out of the subjective (or feeling) and into the objective. An audience will be much more likely to accept a proposed solution to a problem validated by objective evidence and data than they would for one propped up by a feeling or hunch.

Spread the Word

The power of the HES format comes from its specificity and flexibility. The format is specific enough to help women make organized, concise, and well-supported headline statements in an easy-to-follow flow. It safeguards against diluting a main message with multiple modifiers, thereby making it less direct, clear, and effective. It prevents us from overwhelming the audience with too much information (which both women and men do). It's also general enough to be applicable in numerous circumstances. Women who have taken my workshop tell me they use the HES format to make assertions in many different situations, such as meetings, emails, short presentations, performance reviews, and sales pitches.

The power of the HES format comes from its specificity and flexibility.

Based on both my experience and what women tell me, the HES format swiftly becomes a reflex. Women can easily call on it in a moment's notice and in various situations. In using it, they trust they will make a crisp, clear, confident headline statement—and one that is sure not to bury the lede.

In my experience, a large portion of women's anxiety about high-stakes conversations stems from not knowing how to prepare. For this reason, I tell them to share the HES format with other women. We all stand to gain when women are ready and willing to use their voices—confidently, clearly, and effectively.

Anger and the HES Format: A Special Circumstance

We cannot discuss language and power in a book designed to help women communicate effectively in professional settings without also discussing anger. Feeling angry in our work lives is inevitable. It's important to know women must proceed with caution when it comes to expressing anger in professional settings. This is because the expression of anger has implications for women's perceived power—or powerlessness. Women must walk a fine line when choosing language to articulate their anger and using any nonverbal cues to *show* their anger.

In their paper "Can an Angry Woman Get Ahead?" Victoria L. Brescoll, a Yale School of Management faculty member and gender researcher, and Eric Luis Uhlmann, an INSEAD professor and organizational behavior researcher, expose the trap professional women face when communicating anger at work. In the workplace, anger is associated with power and dominance. Given men's socially conferred high social status and their expectation of dominance, they are permitted and expected to convey anger at work, which simultaneously showcases their power and leadership. Given women's lower social status relative to men, they are expected to be subordinate, yielding, and compliant. Therefore, women who are angry in the workplace are violating gendered expectations and are consequently seen as out of control of their emotions and less competent. In addition to paying a reputational price for showing anger, women also risk paying a material price; women who discuss something in job interviews or early in new professional

> Women must proceed with caution when it comes to expressing anger in professional settings.

relationships that made them angry are offered lower wages and accorded less status (i.e., given less power and independence in their work).[1] Once again, women are in a double bind: Leaders are expected to show anger when appropriate, but women are not allowed to show anger in the workplace without potentially paying a price.

In Chapter 3, in which we explored the Contained constraint, I mentioned Soraya Chemaly's research describing how women often (and often unconsciously) transmute their anger into sadness, as it is more socially acceptable for women to be sad. Chemaly argues that society conditions women to interpret and label their anger as sadness. She believes this is by design, as sadness is associated with weakness and powerlessness. While patriarchal society writ large might prefer sad and therefore passive women over angry and proactive women, a patriarchal workplace will also punish women for showing sadness. Women who express sadness in interviews are less likely to be hired. Research on gender stereotypes in the workplace revealed that many professionals expect women to show powerless emotions and be more emotionally dysfunctional.[2] So the mere act of a woman showing sadness in the workplace can affirm the negative biases many of her future or current coworkers may hold of her.

What is an angry woman to do? The research suggests that there are at least two ways women can communicate anger at work without facing backlash:

- Especially in interviews and in the early stages of developing a new professional relationship, it is best to avoid showing anger or sadness, even when needing to discuss an angering or upsetting situation. The research is clear that such expressions of emotion too soon in a professional situation can backfire on women in the form of lower status, power, and pay. However, the research suggests that, with time, women gain some leeway in expressing anger with colleagues who have come to know them on a personal level and are therefore less likely to project on them generalized misogynistic biases.[3]

- When a woman reveals anger at work without explanation, many will assume it is the result of something internal to her and that she is therefore an angry person or emotionally out of control. However, research suggests that when women make a point to attribute their anger to an external or situational cause, it can mitigate the degree of backlash against her. In fact, women can even gain a degree of status and power when using this approach.[4]

Using the HES Format to Express Anger

The HES format helps women avoid the anger trap. In using the HES format to plan your language and practice how you deliver it before a sensitive conversation, you are both supported in making your message strategic and unambiguous, and protected from being unfairly perceived as irrationally or overly emotional.

When using the HES format for avoiding anger, starting with the Foundational Five prompts from Chapter 6 to help you identify your goal and think through the context will take on additional importance. The prompts will help you determine the most appropriate language and tone for what you are trying to accomplish.

As you identify the right mix of language, pay special attention to the power dynamic you want to maintain or achieve through your conversation. There is that fine line to walk, in that you want the person you're addressing to stop or change a behavior, but if your language is too strong, you risk backlash. On the other hand, if your language is not strong enough, the seriousness of your message may be lost on the person with whom you're speaking. Use language that is both sufficiently direct and clear but stops short of being so assertive that it harms you.

Here I'll provide HES examples of expressing anger for three different language strategies: assertive, mixed (assertive/ collaborative), and collaborative. In this example, we'll imagine a scenario where a team leader must confront another team lead about his disrespectful treatment of the speaker's team member, Sarah, in a meeting.

Strategy: **Assertive**

Headline: "I was angry yesterday after observing the way you treated Sarah in the meeting."

Explain: "We agreed a month ago that we would release the report. She sent an email a week ago asking you for preferred dates for the release. My understanding from Sarah is that you did not respond. She took that to mean you did not have a preference. It was unnecessary, in my opinion, to publicly characterize her behavior with derogatory terms like 'sloppy' and 'thoughtless.'"

Support: "I spoke with Sarah and some of the team members. They told me they were uncomfortable with your, and I quote, 'humiliating' language. Sarah was upset, as you might imagine. Everyone, including myself, felt it was a conversation that would have been more appropriate offline. I would like to understand what prompted you to address her that way."

Strategy: **Mixed (Assertive/Collaborative)**

Headline: "I was uncomfortable with how you spoke to Sarah yesterday in front of her direct reports. She did not have a chance to respond, and your language was unusually harsh."

Explain: "I realize you were taken aback, and perhaps that is what prompted a swift and strong response. However, referring to her as 'thoughtless' and 'sloppy' was hurtful to Sarah and undermined her in front of her team."

Support: "I spoke with Sarah and the team. All felt that the conversation was not appropriate for the group setting. Some of the team said they felt bad for Sarah. She would like to discuss it with you first, and then address the issue with the team."

Strategy: **Collaborative**

Headline: "I want to talk about what happened with Sarah yesterday. I was uncomfortable with what you said and how you spoke to her in front of her direct reports. I imagine you had reasons for wanting to confront her in the way that you did, and I want to understand them."

Explain: "Sarah's team had no information about the issue surrounding the release of the report. From my perspective, to raise it in front of the team and expose her seemed unnecessary. Some of the language you used could be perceived as demeaning."

Support: "I spoke with Sarah and some team members. They all felt it was not an appropriate conversation to have in front of the group. They felt bad for Sarah and wanted more information about the incident. I would like to understand what your thinking was so we can resolve it with Sarah and remove any bad feelings between the two of you."

Communicating anger is one of those situations where women must speak and act in a way that directly contradicts our conditioning. However, we know that if we repeatedly dismiss our anger at work, we risk being taken advantage of or missing opportunities.

I have seen so many women deny their anger at work because they have no constructive way to articulate it. Something as simple as the HES format can make a sufficient and positive change in women's ability to respond when they are feeling angry. The HES format puts guardrails on your language and helps you make choices to represent your feelings accurately. And it sets you up to communicate anger productively and effectively, and then feel the enormous relief that follows—the relief of being whole.

CHAPTER 8

Promoting Yourself and Your Accomplishments

Women know that self-promotion is critical to their career advancement, but many don't know how to navigate it effectively. Anytime we want to ask for something we want—more pay, more staff, more resources, a promotion, work-from-home flexibility, and so on—we must justify why we should receive it. This means we must promote ourselves and our accomplishments—something that many women find deeply uncomfortable.

When discussing self-promotion in my *Women, Language, and Power* workshop, I invite a volunteer to role-play a meeting with her manager in which she asks for a raise. Before she begins, I ask her to script out how she will articulate her accomplishments. As she delivers her script, I videotape her so that she can watch it and share her reactions with fellow attendees.

I have done this exercise with hundreds of women. In nearly every case, they are shocked by what they see in the video. They see a woman who lacks confidence, conviction, and clarity. They say things like "I would never give that person a raise!" Or "I look like I don't believe what I'm saying." Or "I look so hesitant and uncomfortable."

These women are not weak, and they do not lack courage. The problem comes from women's cultural conditioning.

Self-promoting language and behavior is less feminine and more masculine. In order to promote themselves, women have to uncomfortably rely on several characteristics of the BSRI masculine scale: taking the calculated risk of being assertive, forceful, ambitious, and willing to take a stand. All of these behaviors run in direct opposition to our training, which tells us not to brag or boast, lest we offend others or fail to consider how it might make them feel.

> **Women's reluctance to self-promote manifests in multiple ways, sometimes extreme and always at a cost to career advancement.**

Women's reluctance to self-promote manifests in multiple ways, sometimes extreme and always at a cost to career advancement:

- *Women will change jobs instead of asking for a raise.* According to a survey of 1,200 employed adults, 57 percent of women have never negotiated their pay. Of the respondents, 60 percent of the women said they would leave their current employer if they could earn more elsewhere. These numbers indicate that a majority of women would rather find a new job than ask for more pay at their current one.[1]

- *If there is no explicit company-wide expectation of negotiation, women won't do it.* A research firm found that men tend to prefer working in organizations where the rules for how salaries are determined are ambiguous or concealed.[2] Whereas men negotiate at greater rates in such organizations, women are deterred by the ambiguity and negotiate less often. By contrast, when the rules of determining pay are transparent in an organization, men and women tend to negotiate in equal numbers.

- *Women will ask for less when negotiating with a male boss than with a female boss.* Today, women are still most likely to work for, and therefore negotiate with, a male boss. If, over the course of a career, women are repeatedly asking for less in negotiations with men, as is suggested by research, women are ultimately paid lower salaries and bonuses compared to men.[3] Women's reluctance to ask for salaries equal to or higher than the salaries of men is at least one factor in the gender pay gap.

- *When women do negotiate, they often do not show up with salary benchmarks to validate their ask.* Gloria Blackwell is a vice president at the American Association of University Women (AAUW), whose mission is to achieve equity for women in the workplace. In her negotiation training sessions for the AAUW, Blackwell found that women tend not to research the salary range for the position they are seeking. This reduces their leverage in negotiations and makes them look unprepared. It also signals to their boss that they don't know what they could be earning, potentially causing the boss to believe he or she can get away with paying them less.

- *When women must describe their accomplishments, they provide less evidence and specificity for them compared to their male peers.* Researchers at the Kelley School of Business recorded interviews of 20 women and 20 men in leadership roles at Fortune 50 companies. The researchers asked each leader, "In your career, what are the accomplishments you are most proud of?" There were several notable differences in how the women and men spoke about their accomplishments. The researchers determined that these differences explain in part why men advance to leadership levels faster and more often.[4]

One of the aspects of self-promotion that the researchers analyzed was how the 20 female and 20 male leaders described their achievements. Culling from the interviews, the researchers identified five categories that leaders used to provide evidence for their accomplishments: 1) use of numbers (e.g., data and percentages); 2) description of positive monetary impact on the company; 3) mentoring or team building; 4) development of products or processes that benefited the company; and 5) position or longevity at the company. The researchers determined that relying on examples from these categories had the effect of adding depth, dimension, and tangibility to the speaker's accomplishments. Of the 40 subjects, 90 percent used information from three or more of these categories to validate and support their accomplishments. Only 45 percent of the women did the same.

- *Women tend to minimize their accomplishments or credit others for their success.* Deborah Tannen found that men are more likely to use "I" when discussing their successes, and women are more likely to use "we."[5] In situations where women must take credit for their achievements in order to justify what they are asking for, the use of "we" serves to undercut their contributions or give undue or disproportionate credit to others.

- *Women believe they must achieve perfection in their current role in order to justify a promotion or more responsibility.* This is a finding from leadership expert Sally Helgesen and leadership coach Marshall Goldsmith in their book *How Women Rise: Break the 12 Habits Holding You Back From Your Next Raise, Promotion, or Job.* Men, by contrast, believe that their potential alone is enough to justify a promotion or more power.[6] The net effect is that women can wait months, even years, before they feel they've performed at a level that warrants self-promotion and justifies more power or pay, while men will "go for it" far earlier in their careers and therefore advance faster than women.

What this list illustrates is the lengths women will go to in order to avoid the discomfort of self-promotion. They would rather wait for someone—usually a preoccupied, busy boss managing his or her own responsibilities, career, and life—to notice all their hard work and hand them more pay, promotions, or other rewards. In *How Women Rise*, Helgesen and Goldsmith document twelve habits that stand in the way of women's career advancement. One troublesome habit most germane to self-promotion is that women expect others to spontaneously notice and reward their contributions.[7]

Women can resent having to promote themselves and their

achievements. In fact, many of my female clients have told me they resent that their work cannot speak for itself and earn them advancement on its own. These women resent that they not only have to exceed expectations to compete with men, but they also have to tell superiors they exceed expectations to get things their male colleagues often already have. They wish their managers would instead pay attention, acknowledge their contributions, and reward them accordingly.

The antidote to discomfort when having to self-promote is a plan.

I have compassion for this frustration. It is true that in order to increase our power, fight for equal pay, get the benefits we deserve, or obtain the resources we need, we have to do things that we've been told our whole lives are unseemly for us to do. It is yet another way that our conditioning leaves us in an unfair double bind.

But I will remind you what I remind my clients. The cold, hard fact remains: If you don't ask, someone else will.

How to Speak About Your Accomplishments

The antidote to discomfort when having to self-promote is a plan. What follows is the script format I provide women who attend my workshop to help them articulate their achievements with sufficient dimension and detail. They are rooted in research and my experience interviewing female and male leaders on this topic.

The format will help you draft a clear and substantive script for self-promotion. Of course, start with the Foundational Five prompts in Chapter 6 to help you identify the appropriate level of assertiveness given your audience and the context. From there, as you think through what to include in your script, keep in mind the importance of describing your successes with depth and specificity. Wherever you can, include evidence of your achievements from these categories:

- Use of numbers
- Positive monetary impact
- Development of products or processes
- Mentoring or team building
- Position and longevity

Self-Promotion Format

In addressing the three essential areas of the format and in the order that follows, you will draft a completed script to promote yourself and your accomplishments.

1) **Describe your accomplishments.** Focus on actions you took and their results. "I" statements must be included here; resist any temptation to use "we" where "I" is warranted.

   Example: "I hit my annual revenue goal of $450,000. Within just six months of managing this new team, we achieved an overall revenue increase of 17 percent compared to last year. We made bringing in new business a priority. As a result, six of the deals I closed were with new clients, ensuring that we will have sustainable growth next year."

2) **Describe the leadership skills you employed in order to achieve your goals.** Possible skills to high-

light include communication/influence, strategic thinking, setting direction, building capability in a team, cross-functional alignment, managing change, project planning, flexibility, mentoring, and giving effective feedback.

Example: "I have shown that I can work cross-functionally to improve the relationship and alignment between the sales and marketing teams. This has decreased the time it takes to get materials customized and produced, which dramatically increased our ability to close deals this year."

3) **Articulate specifically what you are asking for** (e.g., promotion, salary increase, additional head count, larger scope of work, recognition, or working from home). The language you choose for "the ask" must be direct, clear, and concise. If your language is vague, you will appear to lack conviction. You also open the door to a vague response. Use assertive language to close that door. If you are told you cannot get what you want, what else do you want to negotiate for? It is wise to come prepared with scripted language for a secondary ask.

Example: "I have exceeded my goals for the last three quarters as a level six manager. I would like to be put up for senior manager in the upcoming promotion cycle in February."

Things to Keep in Mind as You Script and Self-Promote

Before deciding on what you will ask for, do your research and solicit insights from trusted colleagues who might be able to share good advice. Who before you has received the promotion you want, and what are the company guidelines for the level to which you are hoping to be promoted? What are others earning in the role you want? Who can help you quantify your results? How did others in your company who successfully asked for and received something position or frame their request?

If there are reasons that you feel you cannot ask such questions of coworkers or you need more strategies and tools, I recommend consulting resources from leadership experts or authors. *Pay UP!: Unlocking Insider Secrets of Salary Negotiation* is an excellent book to help prepare for serious conversations about salary. The author—Kate Dixon, a specialist in compensation negotiation—covers terms and concepts crucial to effective negotiation, what to research and how to find salary comparisons, and what to say and not say when asking for more. Part of what makes women uncomfortable about negotiating is the fear that it will turn combative, they will sound selfish, or the relationship with whom they are negotiating could be damaged. Dixon's approach to negotiation is really helpful for women struggling with these concerns and can be summed up in this quote from *Pay UP!:* "When you approach negotiations as a collaborative partnership, where the goal is to have both of you and the company satisfied with the outcome, you're more likely to get what you want."[8]

Once you have a valid justification for the request and a script that lays it out clearly and concisely, practice it as often as you need to in order to deliver it with confidence. Practice in front of others and solicit their feedback. I would also encourage you to record yourself. Observe your nonverbal cues and body language (which you can find detailed guidance on in Chapter 10). Are they all working toward your goal and projecting confidence? Or are they working against your goal? How are you using hand gestures to enhance your language? Are you practicing holding strong and sustained eye contact, especially when you want to drive home a point? Are you sitting up straight and in a posture that projects power? Is your volume commanding? Are you speaking too fast? Have you included a silent pause or two after points where you want to ensure your listener has time to digest? Practice your script until the answer to the question "Would you grant this person her request?" is a "yes."

If you are nervous about self-promoting, question all the assumptions you might hold that would have you believe it is inappropriate or unseemly for you to do. Ask a trusted family member or friend to listen to your concerns and weigh in. Women need help reminding each other how self-defeating it is to let discomfort with self-promotion keep us from the career ambitions, power, pay, and resources we deserve.

CHAPTER 9

Presentations and Public Speaking

I have been teaching presentation skills for over 20 years and have watched thousands of presentations in my workshops and with coaching clients. There is both an art and a science to presenting well, and everyone who is serious about advancement should invest in these skills. In order to help women be as effective as possible when they are presenting, I offer a framework in this chapter that can be used in both formal and informal settings.

At the start of my presentation skills workshop, some participants share that they present more effectively when they don't

The key is knowing what and how to prepare.

prepare speaker notes in advance. They believe this allows them to speak more naturally and avoid sounding scripted. In theory, this notion makes sense, but it is rarely the case that a lack of preparation translates into a more effective delivery. Being able to speak concisely, clearly, and persuasively takes skill, and few people can build these skills without first learning how to prepare. The key is knowing what and how to prepare.

The risks of forgoing preparation go beyond losing your audience in the moment—a lack of preparation can have the much bigger consequence of negatively impacting your career trajectory. Whether you are preparing for a formal presentation, complete with a slide deck and in front of a large audience, or speaking for just a few minutes in a meeting, you have the opportunity to showcase your leadership potential as you present.

A Framework to Create Clear and Convincing Presentations

My career has naturally exposed me to several different public speaking and presentation frameworks. I've used and taught many of them. But I always return to a framework that I made from combining two approaches. When used in conjunction, they offer a simple but comprehensive structure to think through and construct an easy-to-follow, memorable, and well-supported presentation.

The first approach I draw from comes by way of my brother, Michael Baldwin, a former advertising professional and master visual communicator. In his 2015 book, *Just Add Water: An Incredibly Easy Guide for Creating Simple, Powerful Presentations*, he describes the essential question one must answer before creating a presentation: *What is my crystal clear objective?* Meaning, after you've completed the presentation, what do you want your audience to be convinced of about your topic? He points out an important distinction: This is not the same as what you want your audience to *know*. Instead, you want to influence (convince) them to the point of changing an existing belief or developing a new one.[1] Merely having knowledge is passive; holding a belief can incite action.

Thinking through your objective as the first step gives you the advantage of starting with a yardstick against which to measure all content decisions. While the objective is not something you say out loud in your presentation, it puts guardrails on all the content you choose to include and how you choose to present it. If your content does not support the belief you want your audience to hold, then it should be swapped for alternatives that do. As you consider each content option, vet it against your objective.

The second approach I incorporate is from Rick Gilbert and Mary McGlynn's "core message" concept. I add a core message—I use the term "main message"—prompt after establishing the objective. Recall from Chapter 7 that the core message, which I adapted to create the HES format, is a concise, bottom-line assertion that sums up the entire presentation and becomes a mechanism to help audiences remember the main idea. Whether for a five-minute or hour-long presentation, clarifying these two elements—your objective and your main message—is sufficient to develop an outline for your presentation.

My combined framework includes six prompts that help you think through the elements of your presentation; from there, you build out the necessary supporting content. I refer to this framework as the "napkin strategy." There have been several instances where I have been in conference rooms and asked to speak extemporaneously on a topic. I always follow the same plan. I grab a napkin or piece of paper and quickly jot down a bullet point for each of the six prompts. Then, when it's my turn to talk, I take the napkin with me to the front of the room, set it on the table or podium, and glance at it as I speak. For me, the bullet points are key, as they are easier than full sentences to scan as I speak. The framework works equally well when I am planning longer presentations in advance.

Regardless of the nature of the presentation, this framework encourages you to be organized and clear. It allows you to feel relaxed and unrehearsed, instead of nervously reading straight from a script. It's a lightweight but high-impact framework that is so much better than winging it—for you *and* your audience.

Presentation Framework

As you know by now, start with the Foundational Five prompts in Chapter 6 to help you think through appropriate language for your speech before addressing the framework. When drafting responses to the presentation prompts, aim to be as concise as possible. While your responses don't need to literally fit on a napkin, let the napkin strategy remind you that brief is better here. If your answers grow long or unwieldy, it's usually a sign that your objective is not yet clear enough.

I will provide an example from a client who was a designer for an online grocery shopping and delivery service company. Her filled-out framework for a presentation to a group of operations leaders follows.

1) **Objective:** By the end of this presentation, what do I want my audience to believe about my topic?
    Example: Larger-screen devices for in-store shoppers will decrease the number of mistakes they make and thereby increase the number of orders they can fill.

2) **Main message:** How can I distill the objective down to one easy-to-remember sentence?
    Example: Larger-screen devices will save us time and money.

3) **Making the argument:** What content do I need to cover to convince my audience of my objective? As you answer this prompt, consider the audience's preexisting beliefs. Understanding their point of view about your topic will help you shape your argument in order to influence them.

   Example:
   - The always-expanding selection of different brands, sizes, and quantities of products has made in-store shoppers' jobs more complex and slowed their rates of order fulfillment.
   - Smaller-screen devices (mobile phone size) make it hard for shoppers to distinguish the size and brand of a product, exacerbating confusion and leading to mistakes and slower fulfillment rates.
   - Investing in low-cost devices with larger screens will increase revenue.

4) **Support:** What data, examples, or anecdotal evidence could I use to support the content listed in prompt 3?

   Example:
   - The average number of mistakes in-store shoppers make per day
   - What those mistakes cost the company
   - Current number of orders fulfilled daily
   - Projected increase in orders fulfilled daily due to larger-screen devices
   - Cost of larger-screen devices

5) **Opening:** How can I introduce the topic in an interesting

way that supports my message and engages my audience?
Example:

- Show a picture of a half gallon of milk and a quart of milk on the small-screen devices shoppers currently use to illustrate that the products look almost identical.

- Show a picture of a typical in-store display of milk products, which includes an average of 50 different items from which shoppers must select.

- State that an investment in large-screen devices will increase revenue

6) **Closing:** What is my call to action for the audience? As a result of the presentation and their belief in my objective, what specifically do I want them to do?

   Example: I would like your agreement to run a large-screen devices pilot in three stores and compile the data for two weeks, after which we can reconvene and assess the results.

What to Keep in Mind as You Practice Presenting

I know public speaking is terrifying to many. I also know that this anxiety causes too many women to believe they are simply not good presenters and never will be, so they miss out on speaking opportunities that could increase their visibility. But everyone is capable of becoming a strong speaker. I've seen women who fear public speaking grow into masterful presenters. What they eventually come to see is that perfection is not the goal; committing to preparation and practice is. It is the preparation and practice that yield the payoff.

The more prepared you are, the more relaxed and confident

you will feel in front of your audience. Your preparation also signals to your audience that you take yourself and their time seriously, which primes them to be more receptive to your message.

Follow your preparation with practice. Rehearsing your talk out loud is essential if you want to ensure a successful delivery. Especially if this is a high-stakes presentation, practice in front of a colleague or friend. After you've done so, ask them if they were convinced of your objective and if you laid out your argument in a clear and persuasive manner. If they were not convinced, ask them specifically where your argument felt thin or confusing, and make adjustments from there. Finally, ask them if your opening remarks established the main message in an engaging way and if your closing comments conveyed a clear and compelling call to action.

Everyone is capable of becoming a strong speaker.

Plan for and practice your nonverbal cues and body language. As I've previously recommended, record yourself as you practice. Refer to the five categories of nonverbal communication and body language that I lay out in Chapter 10. Let the best practices of each function as a checklist to analyze your hand gestures, eye contact, posture or stance, use of pauses (especially to indicate transitions), and volume.

I encourage you to seek both communications training and as many opportunities to speak publicly as you can. Presentation skills are among the most important skills you can invest in for your career. And there is no shortage of training companies. If your company does not offer presentation skills training, look for ones that offer training to the public. Toastmasters International, for example, is an organization that gathers professionals in weekly meetings to practice public speaking skills for a nominal membership fee. There are also countless books and free online resources on public speaking. I recommend watching the most-viewed TED Talks and studying the speakers—how they organize their presentations, how they move, how they use their bodies and nonverbal cues. Compare the videos you take of yourself to the best and most captivating TED speakers. If you have the opportunity to work with a public speaking coach, by all means take it! A coach will provide you with a range of tools that can help take your presentation skills to the next level.

> Presentation skills are among the most important skills you can invest in for your career.

Some of my clients have created presentation practice groups with female colleagues in their companies. I've also seen these groups form outside of the office. When one of the women in the group has a presentation coming up, other members will volunteer to watch her practice, give notes, and coach her through to a successful presentation day. Women form these groups because they know how important it is to increase their individual and collective visibility. They grasp that the more women there are at the senior levels of their organization, the better off we all will be. And they also appreciate that public speaking is a necessary stepping stone to those senior positions.

Women are strongest when they are each other's advocates and support systems. We must encourage each other to give voice to our ideas and perspectives through public speaking.

In doing so, we create more opportunities for more women to demonstrate their power and rise to senior and leadership levels. And the more women there are in leadership roles, the more women there are who can advocate for yet more women to join them. The larger payoff of supporting each other's development and growth in speaking effectively can literally change the makeup of leaders in our companies and communities.

CHAPTER 10

Cultivating Presence Through Nonverbal Communication and Body Language

Social psychologist Amy Cuddy, who mainstreamed the idea of power posing, and her team stumbled into a disturbing reality about gender and body language. They were in the early stages of launching a study to pinpoint at what age children begin to identify expansive body poses as powerful. In order to conduct their research, they needed some sort of gender-neutral figure to demonstrate poses that are associated with power and poses that are not. They settled on a wooden artist's mannequin (which ended up as the cover model for Cuddy's book, *Presence: Bringing Your Boldest Self to Your Biggest Challenges*).

High-power poses are those where people use their arms and legs to expand out from the torso and take up space. Low-power poses are when people make themselves small and keep their limbs close to their torso. Cuddy and her team manipulated the mannequin into several high-power and low-power poses and took photographs of the mannequin in each one. Prior to diving into the formal study, they test-ran the photographs on their friends' kids to ensure that children could grasp the concept. It was at this point that Cuddy's team discovered children don't think of poses in terms of power, per se; they think of them in terms of gender. Specifically, the children assumed that the photographs with high-power poses were of a male doll, and the photographs with low-power poses were of a female doll.

With this insight, Cuddy and her team changed their plans to study at what age children begin associating high-power poses with boys and low-power poses with girls. Sixty kids—divided into two groups, one of four-year-olds and one of six-year-olds—participated in the study. The team found that 73 percent of the four-year-olds and 85 percent of the six-year-olds held a male-power bias (i.e., an association between power and men), and the rate of bias was more or less the same between the girls and boys. Cuddy and her team also calculated that the six-year-olds were three times more likely than the four-year-olds to think *every* doll in a power pose was male. At age four, kids are well into learning that power is the domain of boys and not of girls. By age six, this lesson is all but locked in.[1]

Knowing what we know about Karin Martin's preschool research from Chapter 3, Cuddy's research makes sense. In the preschool classrooms Martin observed, boys were given near-free rein to be big and take up space as they interacted with others and to be informal and relaxed as they sat. Boys are allowed to comport their bodies in ways that align with what Cuddy and several other researchers have found to be high-power poses. By contrast, girls are taught to comport their bodies in ways that align with what researchers have found to be low-power poses.

In addition to poses, researchers have identified all manner of nonverbal cues and body language that are perceived as either low or high power and status. What and how we communicate

> At age four, kids are well into learning that power is the domain of boys and not of girls. By age six, this lesson is all but locked in.

is undeniably multimodal, in that it is heard in our words and further amplified through our nonverbal communications and body movements. How our words are understood by an audience is heavily influenced by any and all nonverbal cues, including how we use our bodies. These nonverbal cues can enhance our words and engage our audience or contradict our words and lose our audience. The impact of our speaking is a function of all communication modalities coming together. With awareness and practice, we can leverage all modalities to work in concert to amplify our language, broadcast power and high status, and cultivate presence.

The Power of Effective Nonverbal Communication and Body Language

When I am working with clients on presentations, they tell me that they practice by reading over their slides and presenter notes. This is useful only for memorizing the script. This kind of practice will fall short if your goal is to captivate your audience and increase their retention of your ideas. To do this, you must also practice how you will use body language.

Imagine a woman who is giving a boardroom presentation to a senior-level audience about her team's strategy. She stands back from the table, closer to the wall. She doesn't move as she speaks and mostly keeps her hands clasped in front of her waist. Her hand gestures are used only to point to something on the screen displaying her PowerPoint that she wants to highlight. She speaks hastily and in a low volume throughout her entire presentation. Now imagine a woman who starts her presentation by standing directly at the boardroom table. As she speaks, she moves within the space at the front of the room and is sure to sustain strong eye contact with each person in her audience. She uses hand gestures that align with and emphasize key words. Her volume fluctuates when she's making an essential point, and she often follows such points with a pause so that her audience has a moment to digest the information.

We know intuitively which woman conveys confidence and presence and would be most engaging to listen to and watch. Audiences are receptive and responsive to speakers who demonstrate conviction and passion and who attend to them, not just to their speaking notes. When you satisfy this desire, your audience will take you far more seriously, and you will feel deeply gratified.

The goal is to make high-status nonverbal cues and power poses part of your repertoire. When all modes of communication are at your disposal, you stand to make a greater and more memorable impact on your audience—from one person to hundreds. Powerful speakers are perceived as powerful people and listened to accordingly.

The goal is to make high-status nonverbal cues and power poses part of your repertoire.

To get a sense of what I mean, I suggest watching Diana Nyad's first TED Talk. In the early 2010s, you might have read news reports about Nyad. She is known for deciding after her 60th birthday that she wanted to be the first person to complete a continuous swim from Cuba to the Florida Keys without a protective shark cage. Over two years, she made five attempts through dangerous, jellyfish-infested waters to realize her dream.

In her first TED Talk, "Extreme Swimming with the World's Most Dangerous Jellyfish"—given before her final and successful attempt—Nyad explains the agony of her unique and uniquely arduous goal. Her postures, gestures, movements, volume, and pacing are in full alignment with her language, such that they all come together to pull you into her dramatic story. This kind of communication turns an audience into active participants rather than passive listeners. It helps people build the images of the story in their minds. It also helps them empathize with the emotional aspects of the story, making it even more engaging and memorable.

I had the great privilege of once seeing Nyad talk live for an hour. Everyone in the audience was hooked. She had us hanging on every word. Not a phone was checked. Not a bathroom break was taken. We were transfixed and transported into her world, and we didn't want to leave.

How to Use the Five Forms of Nonverbal Communication and Body Language

There are five forms of nonverbal communication and body language that we can leverage to connect with our audience, enrich our message, and project power and presence: hand gestures, eye contact, postures and poses, pausing, and volume. Be aware that all of these forms of nonverbal communication and body language interrelate and tend to influence and play off of each other.

To optimize their benefits, apply the best practices of each to culminate in an engaging, high-impact conversation or speech.

Form 1: Hand Gestures
Hand gestures are not meaningless movements. Research has

shown that hand gestures can carry between 50 and 70 percent of the information encoded in a speaker's message.[2] Our hand gestures add significant weight and meaning to our words—and this weight and meaning can enhance or detract from our language depending on how we use our gestures.

When hand gestures emphasize our words and animate our speaking patterns, audiences listen to and retain more of what we say. Gestures also have the added benefit of naturally causing variations in vocal volume. When you use your hand to emphasize a word—for example, raising your hand up as high as your neck as you say the word "increase"—you will naturally speak that word slightly louder than if you did not gesture. Gestures are a great asset to speakers who would otherwise speak in the same volume for all words.

Gestures can even influence decision-making. A research team out of a Netherlands university asked experienced investors to watch one of four videos of an entrepreneur pitching a new device. In only one of the videos did the entrepreneur use hand gestures. The investors who watched this video were 12 percent more interested in investing than those who watched presenters who did not use hand gestures.[3]

> **When hand gestures emphasize our words and animate our speaking patterns, audiences listen to and retain more of what we say.**

Effective hand gestures also make people more likely to want to listen to our words. A human behavior research team analyzed the most- and least-watched TED Talks of all time and found a correlation between hand gestures and viewership. The least-watched TED speakers used about 272 hand gestures in the average 18-minute TED Talk. By contrast, the most viral TED speakers used an average of 465 hand gestures in their 18 minutes.[4]

That said, it's not enough simply to gesticulate. Body language expert Carol Kinsey Goman has found through her extensive analysis that when people's hand gestures contradict their words, audiences are less likely to trust them.[5]

By contrast, alignment between words and gestures makes a person appear trustworthy and even warm and agreeable.[6] Additional research has shown that an average of 14 gestures per minute increases one's persuasiveness, as long as the gestures are "illustrative," "ideational," and correlated to language.[7]

To harness the power of hand gestures, follow these best practices:

- *Use hand gestures that align with your words.* For example, if you are referring to "peaks and valleys" in your sales forecast but your hand moves in front of your body in a flat line, you will trigger cognitive dissonance in your audience and lose their trust. Instead, a hand gesture to draw larger and clear "ups and downs" in the space to one side of your body illustrates your message while fostering trust.
- *Use large gestures to emphasize key words.* As an example, if you are saying that the candidate for the open SVP role is "*totally* unprepared," a wide gesture where you start with both hands in front of you and then sweep them far out to either side of your body will emphasize "totally." As a result, listeners will pay more attention to the point you are trying to make through use of the word "totally."

Without a gesture, the word might not stand out and its importance could be lost.

- *Avoid indiscriminate or rapid gesturing.* Gestures that don't align with words begin to feel discordant and will impair the audience's comprehension. Gestures that are too rapid feel chaotic to the audience and distract from the speaker's words.

- *Avoid an over-reliance on the same few gestures.* Audiences tend to lose interest when aspects of a speaker's verbal or nonverbal communication default to a pattern. Many presenters have the same two or three gestures they use repeatedly. Audiences will quickly recognize this as a pattern and begin to lose interest in the speaker.

- *Plant your feet hip-width apart to support effective gesturing.* If our bodies are unbalanced, our gestures will be smaller. Standing with both feet squarely on the ground and the width of your hips will not only make you appear grounded and confident, it will also make you *feel* grounded and confident. When wearing too-high heels, standing with one leg crossed over the other, or standing with one knee cocked, you won't have the balance you need to capture the benefit of the most effective gestures.

Form 2: Eye Contact

A speaker's eye contact can influence how an audience interprets the information she relays and the action they might take with it. Research has shown that when a speaker makes direct eye contact with a listener, the listener will relate the information she is hearing to her own experience.[8] This has the effect of amplifying the listener's comprehension and memory of the new information, and the information is more likely to be automatically incorporated into the listener's future decision-making.

In an informal survey of 22 executives I interviewed about the importance of nonverbal communication in professional settings, nearly all of them ranked strong eye contact as the form they deem most important. To them, eye contact signals confidence and credibility, and a lack of it signals the opposite. As a representative example, one executive said, "If someone can't look me in the eye when they are making a point, it indicates to me that they are not confident about what they are saying, and I can't trust what they are saying."

> A speaker's eye contact can influence how an audience interprets the information she relays and the action they might take with it.

Making strong eye contact with those in your audience can feel awkward at first. But it's a must to push through the discomfort in order to achieve its benefits.

In addition to boosting your credibility and influence, strong eye contact with your audience provides three more benefits:

1) *Eye contact slows you down.* Most people speak too fast. Audiences can read this as nervousness and a lack of confidence. In addition to coaching women to use hand gestures that will slow their speaking pace, I also guide them to make eye contact with audience members. When we make eye contact, we naturally slow down our speech. This is because it is unnatural to speak at an accelerated pace to an individual person. When we hold eye contact with one person, we tend to slow our speech to the typical pace of one-on-one conversation.

2) *Eye contact calms your nerves.* When we speak too fast, we are more prone to tripping over our words. In using eye contact to slow down our speech, we can regain a sense of control over our language, which in turn reduces anxiety. It has been shown that eye contact of at least three to five seconds calms the nerves of the speaker.[9] The trick is allowing yourself to push past that initial awkwardness and grow comfortable sustaining eye contact long enough to benefit from its calming effect.

3) *Eye contact can increase vocal variation.* I've observed this on countless occasions—when speakers make sustained eye contact with individuals in the audience, their voice naturally becomes more varied in tone, inflection, and volume. Speaking in monotone is not natural in typical conversations; when we're speaking with a colleague or friend, our speech is filled with vocal variation—even without our conscious effort. Similar to how sustained eye contact with one audience member slows down your speech, it also restores the vocal variation that would be there if you were in a one-on-one conversation with that person. When speakers only rapidly scan an audience without stopping to hold eye contact with and speak to individuals, they sacrifice vocal variation and audience interest.

For both you and your audience to reap the rewards of strong eye contact, follow these best practices:

- *Commit to eye contact long enough to gain its benefits.* In my workshops, I will ask volunteers to give short presentations to practice various speaking skills. When a volunteer is practicing holding eye contact while speaking, the audience invariably remarks that the speaker's eye contact boosted their engagement. Similarly, the speakers almost always report that they can observe and feel the audience's increased engagement, which has the instantaneous effect of making them more confident. Keep in mind that even if *you* feel self-conscious holding eye contact for a full sentence, you will appear less nervous and more confident to your *audience.*

- *When you want to emphasize a point, hold eye contact with one person for the entire time you are making that point.* I'll go into more detail on how to do this in the next bullet point. What's important to know first is that eye contact with one audience member does not make others feel excluded. Instead, sustained eye contact with an individual signals to everyone in the audience that what you're saying warrants their close attention.

- *Utilize both audience scanning and individual eye contact.* I call this tactic "scan and land." Scan the entire audience when you are speaking until you reach an important sentence you want to emphasize. Just before you speak this sentence, stop scanning and hold eye contact with one person for the full sentence. If it's a longer sentence or the next sentence also requires emphasis, shift to a second person and hold eye contact for the duration of the point you want to drive home. As we know, sustained eye contact will bring forth the benefits of slowed pace and vocal variation. It also signals your conviction in the point and gives your audience a moment to think about and consider what you have said. Then, you can resume scanning—repeating the process again for each sentence you want to accentuate.

Form 3: Posture and Posing

Goman, the body language expert, often says that confidence when speaking is displayed in "height and space."[10] As a general rule, you want to stand or sit tall (height) and expand your arms out from the sides of your torso (space) when gesturing. This can feel unnatural to those of us who were trained as girls to make ourselves as small and unimposing as possible. But as long as we remain stuck in contained postures, we risk projecting a lack of confidence in the words we are speaking.

> Goman, the body language expert, often says that confidence when speaking is displayed in "height and space."

Best posture and posing practices when standing include:

- If presenting in a room with a table, stand directly at the front of the table. Place your feet hip-width apart, as this stance is associated with power and confidence. Begin with your hands dropped to your sides until you start speaking, at which point you can incorporate hand gestures. Taking this power pose commands your audience's focus and communicates that you are comfortable in the spotlight.

- When speaking with a PowerPoint presentation, do not let the slides become the focus of your talk. Anytime you do not need your audience focused on a slide, you want them focused on you. To draw their attention from the screen and back to you, step forward or somewhat away from the screen so that their eyes follow you. Or temporarily blank the screen while you finish your point, turning the slides back on only when needed.

- Remember the role that clothing plays in your ability to move. Opt for clothing that enables free movement and the balance needed to hold powerful poses.

- When speaking at a lectern, step to the side of it to speak once your presentation begins. If that's not possible for the duration of your speech, step to the side of it when you want to add emphasis to important points and then return to the lectern. When behind the lectern, hand gestures take on even more importance. Often, speakers will hold onto the sides of a podium, which eliminates any gestures—so avoid doing this!

Best posture and posing practices when sitting include:

- Even when sitting, it's important to create a presence by sitting up tall and taking up space with gestures. Sit up straight in the chair with your head held high. To the extent that you can, put both feet on the floor with your legs and ankles uncrossed, as crossed ankles are associated with low status. Sit at the edge of your chair to signal that you are paying attention and are ready for conversation. Make sure your shoulders are upright and back, not rounded or slouched.

- Make your hands visible to your audience as often and naturally as possible, which might require occasionally resting one or both hands on a desk or table in front of you. Remember to use gestures that illustrate and amplify your language.

- In more informal settings, it's OK and sometimes even beneficial to sit in a more open and relaxed position. Recall the male client I mentioned at the start of Chapter 3 who sat on a panel with another man and a woman. The woman's tight, short dress required that she tuck herself in to avoid giving the audience a view up her dress. Meanwhile, the men—in their pants and casual shirts—were free to lean back in a relaxed pose when not speaking, lean forward when they were, and change their position whenever it felt appropriate to them. In less formal settings, less formal clothing can enable the more expansive and relaxed seated positions that men so often use to express ease and confidence.

General best practices for poses and postures include the following:
- An upright and straight neck shows confidence and power. That said, when it's advantageous to show empathy, tilt your head slightly.
- Women tend to nod too much, while men tend to nod only when they want to indicate agreement with a speaker.[11] As you listen, avoid nodding for no reason, as this can distract your audience.
- When appropriate, turn your whole body toward the person you are speaking to. This will cause them to pay more attention to you and what you are saying.

Form 4: Pausing

President Barack Obama is known to many as a great orator. His speaking skills are numerous but, in my opinion, one stands above the rest: his mastery of the pause.

Pauses pack serious punch. They are one of the most powerful ways to demonstrate your confidence and your authority. It takes confidence to pause for a few seconds—and your audience knows this. Inserting a silent pause after you make a point says to the audience that you believe your point is important enough to give them a moment to ponder it. Pauses can also be strategically used to underscore the words that preceded them. Furthermore, pauses support an audience's working memory, which is the short-term memory function we use to temporarily hold what we are learning as our brains attempt to assimilate and understand new information. If something is to make it to our long-term memories, it must be sustained long enough in our working memory first. By allowing listeners' working memories a moment to process new information without also simultaneously taking in additional information, pauses have a material and positive impact on your audience's cognitive processing and ultimate comprehension and recall of your point.[12]

> **Pauses pack serious punch. They are one of the most powerful ways to demonstrate your confidence and your authority.**

Pauses also provide a benefit to you, the speaker. They can offer the opportunity for you to take a deep breath and calm any nerves. Or you can use the break to regroup, collect your thoughts, and get back on track if you've lost your place. Pauses are also a simple way to transition to your next point.

While deliberate and premeditated pauses are more likely to

be used in speeches, pauses offer similar benefits in conversation. A study found that a pause even as short as a half a second boosted listener retention of the sentences or thoughts surrounding them. The trick in dialogue is to avoid a pause longer than four seconds. Anything beyond this threshold is perceived as unusual and can confuse your audience or cause them to think you've lost your train of thought.[13] The point is not to fear pauses when they happen naturally in your speech or rush to fill them, as their use is supporting the audience's comprehension of your point and helping you project confidence.

To unlock the benefits of the powerful pause, follow these best practices:

- Whenever drafting a script for a high-stakes conversation, speech, or presentation, account for pauses. Determine where in your speech you want to pause and then place a symbol, such as a slash, accordingly in your presenter notes. In addition to using pauses for emphasis, also use them to transition to a new point and especially a new segment of your speech.
- As you begin incorporating pauses into your communication repertoire, start with shorter pauses and build up to pauses lasting three or four seconds.
- Clients often ask me what they're supposed to do during a pause. I suggest they count the seconds. Or I tell them to scan the room (or, if on a video conference, look into the camera). Sometimes I look at one person during the pause. President Obama often looks away into the distance during his pauses. There is no right answer except to do whatever makes you comfortable during the pause.

Form 5: Volume

In my workshops, I will invite a participant to the front of the room to speak a few sentences at her typical volume. I then ask the audience to rate the speaker's volume as low (i.e., a volume that is difficult to hear without straining), adequate (i.e., a volume that is sufficient to be heard), or commanding (i.e., an authoritative volume that draws in the audience and compels them to listen closely to the speaker). In almost every instance, the audience reports that the speaker's volume is low or adequate. So I ask the speaker to repeat the same sentences, but this time in a louder voice. And we repeat this process until the audience reports that they can not only hear the speaker clearly, but that they are also compelled to give the speaker their undivided attention. It usually takes a few attempts before the speaker is speaking at a volume that the audience deems "commanding." In nearly every case, the speaker comments that this volume genuinely feels like yelling.

> It takes practice to achieve and grow comfortable using the volume of voice that commands attention.

When it comes to typical conversation, we are familiar with speaking at the volume that ensures we are heard. It takes practice to achieve and grow comfortable using the volume of voice that commands attention.

From there, volume must be varied as you speak in order to continue to maintain your audience's interest. Even if a volume is loud enough to grab the audience's attention, if it never fluctuates, it will fail to hold the audience's attention or interest for long. Increase your volume when you want to emphasize an important word or point.

Best practices for achieving a commanding and interesting use of volume include the following:

- Reaching a commanding volume is particularly difficult for women who've been conditioned to contain their voices and fear sounding too loud. It is also something we typically cannot achieve on our own. As you work to find this volume, rely on others to tell you when you've achieved it. Once others have helped you pinpoint your authoritative volume, practice speaking at this volume again and again until it begins to feel less strange and, eventually, normal.

- Variation in volume is often a function of hand gestures. Recall that using hand gestures naturally causes a slight uptick in your volume. If you are not frequently using a range of small and large gestures to emphasize certain words, you will also likely be speaking in a more consistent, and therefore less engaging and interesting, volume.

What to Keep in Mind as You Prepare and Practice

Let this chapter be a resource for you. Refer back to it as you build a habit of planning and practicing nonverbal communication and body language that will bring conviction and interest to your words and help you cultivate presence.

Take advantage of the incredible technologies at our disposal. Videotaping yourself—through your phone, Zoom, or an app—is by far one of the most powerful ways to improve. Areas that need additional refinement or practice will become obvious to you. Alternatively, you can view the video with someone you trust to give you honest feedback. Watching a video helps you see what the audience sees, and it might be very different from what you worry the audience will see. For high-stakes conversations, I advise clients to practice with a trusted colleague or friend.

There are scores of books available on the topics of public speaking and high-impact body language and nonverbal communication. There are also countless free resources online. I encourage you to watch voice and presence expert Hillary Wicht's TEDx Talk, "From Battle of the Sexes to Balance of the Sexes," which is full of great tips to keep in mind as you prepare and practice.

Achieving the level of presence and power that comes from using all modes of communication when you speak can, at first, feel uncomfortable. As you push through the discomfort to un-contain your body, remember that you were born to take up space and express yourself through body language. The conditioning that made us believe otherwise is not truth. Just like using your full language repertoire, using your whole body to communicate with conviction and convey your power is your truth. And once you restore it, you will feel at home.

Afterword

When President Obama first took office in 2009, two-thirds of his top advisers and staffers were men. According to a 2016 article in *The Washington Post* by Juliet Eilperin, female aides were often left out of key meetings and complained that they had to fight to be included in "the room where it happened."[1] Once there, they felt ignored, talked over, steamrolled, and dismissed. If they managed to express an idea without a man interrupting them, the men would often claim it as their own.

Having had enough, the women met as a group and decided to use a strategy they called "amplification." They agreed that, in every meeting and conversation, they would publicly support, reinforce, and give each other credit for their ideas. In practice, amplification looks like this: If a man interrupts Nikkia in a meeting, Lynee will interrupt the man and say, "I'd like to hear what Nikkia was saying because her point is important." If a man claims an idea was his when it was in fact Renee's, Nikkia will immediately say, "That's a great idea—I recall that Renee was the one who initially brought it to our attention." If Barbara says, "I recommend that we aim for a February rollout of the program," Ursula will chime in with "I second Barbara's recommendation."

The women of the Obama administration did not relent, and they amplified each other every chance they had. Eventually, the men—including Obama himself—caught on. They proactively sought the women's perspectives and ideas. The women were able to speak more frequently and without being interrupted. And the men took their ideas and recommendations as seriously as they had always taken each other's.

The women's simple strategy worked. The time they had reclaimed to express their ideas had a material impact on the policies that the Obama administration put forward, including but not limited to an equal pay policy, an expanded Small Business Administration lending to female entrepreneurs, and policies to attract, retain, and promote more women in STEM (science, technology, engineering, and mathematics). It also led to an increase in female hires, such that by the end of Obama's second term, there was an equal number of men and women in his inner circle.

This is how we create a culture—in the office and beyond—of women supporting women in our individual and collective rise to power. It is how we help other women's voices and ideas get heard, taken seriously, and acted upon.

We can make advancements when we go it alone. But we can go so much further together. Because as and more of us:

> demand to be heard,
>
> assert our needs,
>
> speak loudly with conviction,
>
> expand our bodies and take up space,
>
> express our rightful indignation and require change,
>
> take ourselves seriously and insist that others do the same,

the more we can effect real change for ourselves and all women.

Each time we dare to defy our feminine conditioning, we engage in a small act of protest with big payoff. As we work toward continued structural changes to achieve women's full equality, we can work these daily acts of protest into our language and behaviors to shift the power dynamics around us.

Thank you for joining me in this most important conversation and for reading this book. I hope you experience the sense of liberation and excitement that I see in my clients and the women in my workshops. I hope you meet aspects of yourself you didn't know you had but are thrilled to find. I hope you discover reservoirs of gumption, confidence, and courage that have gone untapped and hidden from your view for too long. I hope that your sense of wholeness, your agency, and a promise to self-advocate become the forces that drive your decisions and turn your ambitions into realities.

There is one thing I can say for sure about my years of work with women: They repeatedly leave me in awe. Women have a strength, resilience, adaptability, intelligence, compassion, and empathy that inspires me daily. Thank you for giving meaning and hope to the work I do.

I wish you the best of luck. May you do great things.

—Susannah

References

Part One

Chapter 1

1. Betty Friedan, *The Feminine Mystique* (New York: W. W. Norton, 1963).

2. Anna Fels, *Necessary Dreams: Ambition in Women's Changing Lives* (South Shore, MA: Anchor, 2005).

3. Fels, *Necessary Dreams*, 19.

4. Fels, *Necessary Dreams*, 24.

5. Fels, *Necessary Dreams*, 39.

6. Robin Tolmach Lakoff, *Language and Woman's Place: Text and Commentaries (Studies in Language and Gender)*. Rev. and expanded ed. Edited by Mary Bucholtz. (New York: Oxford University Press, 2004).

Chapter 2

1. Herminia Ibarra, Robin J. Ely, and Deborah M. Kolb, "Women Rising: The Unseen Barriers," *Harvard Business Review* (September 2013).

2. Ibarra, Ely, and Kolb, "Women Rising."

3. Sandra Bem, "The Measurement of Psychological Androgyny," *Journal of Consulting and Clinical Psychology*, Vol. 42, No. 2 (1974), 155-162.

4. Deborah Ballard-Reisch and Mary Elton, "Gender Orientation and

the Bem Sex Role Inventory: A Psychological Construct Revisited," *Sex Roles*, Vol. 27, 291-306.

5. Rachel Simmons, *The Curse of the Good Girl: Raising Authentic Girls With Courage and Confidence* (New York: Penguin, 2009), 1.

6. Simmons, *The Curse of the Good Girl*, 1-2.

7. Girl Scout Research Institute, *Change It Up! What Girls Say About Redefining Leadership*, 2008.

8. Simmons, *The Curse of the Good Girl*, 3.

9. Alicia Menendez, *The Likeability Trap: How to Break Free and Succeed as You Are* (New York: Harper Business, 2019).

10. Kimberly Fitch and Sangeeta Agrawal, "Why Women Are Better Managers Than Men," *Gallup Business Journal* (October 16, 2014).

11. Madeline E. Heilman, Aaron S. Wallen, Daniella Fuchs, and Melinda M. Tamkins, "Penalties for Success: Reactions to Women Who Succeed at Male Gender-Typed Tasks," *Journal of Applied Psychology*, Vol. 89, No. 3 (2004): 416-27.

12. Heilman, Wallen, Fuchs, and Tamkins, "Penalties for Success: Reactions to Women Who Succeed at Male Gender-Typed Tasks."

13. Corinne Moss-Racusin, "Understanding Women's Self-Promotion Detriments: The Backlash Avoidance Model" (dissertation), https://rucore.libraries.rutgers.edu/rutgers-lib/33951/PDF/1/play.

Chapter 3

1. Karin A. Martin, "Becoming a Gendered Body: Practices of Preschools," *American Sociological Review*, Vol. 63, No. 4 (1998), 494-511.

2. Martin, "Becoming a Gendered Body: Practices of Preschools."

3. Martin, "Becoming a Gendered Body: Practices of Preschools."

4. Soraya Chemaly, *Rage Becomes Her: The Power of Women's Anger* (New York: Atria Books, 2019), xxi.

5. Chemaly, *Rage Becomes Her*, 7.

6. Chemaly, *Rage Becomes Her*, 5.

7. Chemaly, *Rage Becomes Her*, xxi.

8. Lia Karsten, "Children's Use of Public Space: The Gendered World of the Playground," *Childhood*, Vol. 10, No. 4 (2003), 457-473.

9. Barrie Thorne, *Gender Play: Girls and Boys in School* (New Brunswick, NJ: Rutgers University Press, 1993), 83.

10. Myra Sadker and David Sadker, *Failing at Fairness: How Our Schools Cheat Girls* (New York: Scribner, 1995), 43.

11. American Association of University Women, *How Schools Short-change Girls: The AAUW Report: A Study of Major Findings on Girls and Education* (New York: Marlowe & Co., 1995).

12. Daniel Voyer and Susan D. Voyer, "Gender Differences in Scholastic Achievement: A Meta-Analysis," *Psychological Bulletin*, Vol. 140, No. 4 (2014), 1174-1204.

13. Valerie Fridland, "Why Do We Think Women Talk Too Much?" *Psychology Today* (July 12, 2020).

14. Gary Fountain, "Study Shows Benefits of All-Girls Schools," *Richmond Times-Dispatch* (April 26, 2009).

15. Sylvia Ann Hewlett, *Executive Presence: The Missing Link Between Merit*

and Success (New York: Harper Business, 2014), 5-6.

16. Hewlett, *Executive Presence*, 6.

17. Hewlett, *Executive Presence*, 7.

18. Shelley J. Correll and Lori Nishiura Mackenzie, "To Succeed in Tech, Women Need More Visibility," *Harvard Business Review* (September 13, 2016).

19. Jenna Goudreau, "Do You Have 'Executive Presence'?" *Forbes* (October 29, 2012).

20. Goudreau, "Do You Have 'Executive Presence'?"

21. Anett D. Granta and Amanda Taylor, "Communication Essentials for Female Executives to Develop Leadership Presence: Getting Beyond the Barriers of Understating Accomplishment," *Business Horizons*, Vol. 57, No. 1 (2014), 73-83.

22. Iris Marion Young, "Throwing Like a Girl: A Phenomenology of Feminine Body Comportment Motility and Spatiality," *Human Studies*, Vol. 3, No. 2 (1980), 137-156.

23. Young, "Throwing Like a Girl: A Phenomenology of Feminine Body Comportment Motility and Spatiality."

24. Amy Cuddy, "My Overview of the State of the Science on Postural Feedback ('Power Posing'), and Some Comments on Civilized Scientific Discourse," LinkedIn (October 4, 2016).

Chapter 4

1. Deborah Tannen, "The Power of Talk: Who Gets Heard and Why," *Harvard Business Review* (September-October 1995).

2. Tannen, "The Power of Talk."

3. Carole Edelsky, "Who's Got the Floor?" *Language in Society*, Vol. 10, No. 3 (1981): 383-421.

4. Edelsky, "Who's Got the Floor?"

5. Lakoff, "Language and Woman's Place."

6. Deborah Tannen, *Talking From 9 to 5: Women and Men at Work* (New York: William Morrow & Company, 1994), 132.

7. Granta and Taylor, "Communication Essentials for Female Executives to Develop Leadership Presence."

8. Granta and Taylor, "Communication Essentials for Female Executives to Develop Leadership Presence."

9. Fitch and Agrawal, "Why Women Are Better Managers Than Men."

10. Judith Baxter, "How Speech and Language Determine Success in the Workplace," *The Guardian* (June 3, 2013).

11. Baxter, "How Speech and Language Determine Success in the Workplace."

Part Two

A Note on Part Two

1. Nick Drydakis, Katerina Sidiropoulou, Swetketu Patnaik, Sandra Selmanovic, and Vasiliki Bozani, "Masculine vs. Feminine Personality Traits and Women's Employment Outcomes in Britain: A Field Experiment," *International Journal of Manpower*, Vol. 39, No. 4 (2018), 621-630.

Chapter 7

1. Victoria L. Brescoll and Eric Luis Uhlmann, "Can an Angry Woman Get Ahead? Status Conferral, Gender, and Expression of Emotion in the Workplace," *Psychological Science*, Vol. 19, No. 3 (2008), 268-275.

2. Jacqueline S. Smith, "Constrained by Emotion: Women, Leadership, and Expressing Emotion in the Workplace," *Handbook on Well-Being of Working Women* (2016), 209-224.

3. Brescoll and Uhlmann, "Can an Angry Woman Get Ahead?"

4. Brescoll and Uhlmann, "Can an Angry Woman Get Ahead?"

Chapter 8

1. Randstad, "Salary and Compensation Statistics on the Impact of COVID-19," https://rlc.randstadusa.com/for-business/learning-center/future-workplace-trends/randstad-2020-compensation-insights.

2. Andreas Leibbrandt and John A. List, "Do Women Avoid Salary Negotiations? Evidence From a Large Scale Natural Field Experiment," National Bureau of Economic Research Working Paper Series, November 2012.

3. Iñigo Hernandez-Arenaza and Nagore Iriberri, "Women Ask for Less (Only From Men): Evidence From Bargaining in the Field," *Journal of Economic Behavior & Organization*, Vol. 152 (2018), 192-214.

4. Granta and Taylor, "Communication Essentials for Female Executives to Develop Leadership Presence."

5. Tannen, "The Power of Talk."

6. Sally Helgesen and Marshall Goldsmith, *How Women Rise: Break the 12 Habits Holding You Back from Your Next Raise, Promotion, or Job* (New

York: Hachette, 2018), 128.

7. Helgesen and Goldsmith, *How Women Rise*, 76.

8. Kate Dixon, *Pay UP!: Unlocking Insider Secrets of Salary Negotiation* (Oceanside Press, 2020).

Chapter 9

1. Michael Baldwin, *Just Add Water: An Incredibly Easy Guide for Creating Simple, Powerful Presentations* (Oakland, CA: Inkshares, 2015).

Chapter 10

1. Amy Cuddy, *Presence: Bringing Your Boldest Self to Your Biggest Challenges* (New York: Little, Brown Spark, 2018).

2. Judith Holler, Kobin H. Kendrick, and Stephen C. Levinson, "Processing Language in Face-to-Face Conversation: Questions With Gestures Get Faster Responses," *Psychonomic Bulletin & Review*, Vol. 25 (2018), 1900-1908.

3. Nicole Torres, "When You Pitch an Idea, Gestures Matter More Than Words," *Harvard Business Review* (May-June 2019).

4. Vanessa Van Edwards and Brandon Vaughn, "5 Secrets of a Successful TED Talk," Science of People (March 3, 2015).

5. Carol Kinsey Goman, "5 Ways Body Language Impacts Leadership Results," *Forbes* (August 26, 2018).

6. Carolyn Gregoire, "The Fascinating Science Behind 'Talking' With Your Hands," *Huffington Post* (February 4, 2016).

7. Granta and Taylor, "Communication Essentials for Female Executives to Develop Leadership Presence."

8. Laurence Conty, Nathalie George, and Jari K. Hietanen, "Watching Eyes Effects: When Others Meet the Self," *Consciousness and Cognition*, Vol. 45 (2016), 184-197.

9. Dom Barnard, "The Importance of Eye Contact During a Presentation," Virtual Speech blog (October 24, 2017).

10. "Carol Kinsey Goman: Body Language for Business Women," YouTube, https://www.youtube.com/watch?v=hShW4jhSqNE (June 26, 2019).

11. "Carol Kinsey Goman: Body Language for Business Women," YouTube.

12. Lucy J. MacGregor, Martin Corley, and David I. Donaldson, "Listening to the Sound of Silence: Disfluent Silent Pauses in Speech Have Consequences for Listeners," *Neuropsychologia*, Vol. 48, No. 14 (2010), 3982-3992.

13. University of Gothenburg, "Pauses Can Make or Break a Conversation," ScienceDaily (September 30, 2015).

Afterword

1. Juliet Eilperin, "White House Women Want to Be in the Room Where It Happens," *Washington Post* (September 13, 2016).

About the Author

Susannah Baldwin, Ph.D., is an executive and communications coach who combines her experience as a clinical psychologist with extensive corporate expertise to help clients hone the necessary skills to lead diverse teams in demanding environments.

She began her career in a leadership development consulting firm, where she focused on building collaborative leadership skills with leaders in Fortune 50 companies. In developing those collaborative workplaces, she implemented large-scale corporate initiatives, designed and facilitated strategic and operational planning meetings, and coached emerging and senior leaders.

Baldwin's recognition that communication is a critical skill for leadership led her to leave consulting and move into the area of leadership communication coaching. During that time, she coached leaders and executives for high-stakes presentations and to gain the communication skills needed for their career stage.

Since 2010, Baldwin has been focused on executive and communication coaching with a special focus on women's advancement. Applying her research from clinical psychology, Baldwin shows women how to recognize the ways in which they circumscribe their own power and instead align their language and communication choices with their purpose, power, and ambition.

Baldwin is also a master trainer in the area of communication skills. She and a team of associates deliver a variety of workshops on communication—including *Present with Impact*, *Storytelling That Sells*, *Selling to Senior Leaders*, and *Women, Language, and Power*. Baldwin is an experienced public speaker, moderator, and weekly radio show host.

susannahbaldwin.com